JOURNEY INTO GLORY

GEORG KARL

ENDORSEMENTS

I always consider it an honor and a privilege to write an endorsement for a book when its central message is one that resonates in my own spirit. Such is the case with Pastor Georg Karl's new book, "Journey into Glory". An important message it conveys is, in essence, that the Gospel of the Kingdom is not merely a historical gospel; rather, the Word of God is alive, real, and active today (Hebrews 4:12). In the beginning, God created mankind in eternity within the atmosphere of His Glory, later revealed that Glory on earth through the person of Jesus Christ, and today invites us to become carriers of the Glory and manifest it for the world to experience.

God is using Pastor Karl, along with his wife Irina, to expand the Gospel of the Kingdom of God that Jesus Christ preached and demonstrated in Germany, as well as internationally. Pastor Karl makes the point that the Great Commission of God, given to us by Jesus, can only be carried out effectively by the supernatural power of the Holy Spirit. With the sense of urgency that comes once we discern that Jesus will soon return, the Body of Christ must know that we are all called to be witnesses of Jesus - as the sons and daughters of God of all ages, races, and nationalities - that not only speak of Him but that also demonstrate His Glory and power in a tangible way through salvation, transformation, healing, deliverance, miracles, signs and wonders of every kind. I recommend this book, "Journey into Glory", to leaders and church members alike as the revelation in this book, received and applied by faith, will undoubtedly touch, change, and transform the lives of all who receive it.

Apostle Guillermo Maldonado
King Jesus International Ministry
Miami, FL

It is a joy for me to endorse Pastor Karl's wonderful book on the subject of the Glory of God! You will be blessed and inspired to seek God on a much deeper level in your life as you read this book.

Bobby Conner
Eagles View Ministry

I want to highly recommend to you this amazing book "journey into glory" by my good friend Georg Karl. Georg is a revivalist that carries an incredible revelation on not only how to move in the Glory but an understanding and IMPARTATION on how the Glory works. If you are hungry for the miraculous and have a desire to move in the deep things of God then this book is for you.

Jeff Jansen
Global Fire Ministries International
Senior Leader of Global Fire Church
Author of Glory Rising/Furious Sound of Glory

This book is on the cutting edge of what God is doing today in this fresh move of God's Glory Harvest across the earth! I have personally ministered with Georg both in his congregation and on the streets with him in Germany as the atmosphere of the glory he has developed in his life and ministry made it easy to flow in the supernatural glory of God with signs following and souls saved.

I can truly say that he is the 'real deal' and a true friend having also spent time together in each other's home and praying often for each other.

Very few carry the true Glory of God on the earth as he does.

I can personally attest to the love, joy, Christlikeness, the faith, healings, signs and wonders and Glory that flow freely from Georg and his wife Irina.

I have lived and ministered in the glory for many years yet I was so blessed and refreshed reading this book I could not put it down and read it almost entirely in one reading. No matter how long you've known the Lord, this is a must read for anyone that wants to be part of this fresh new move of God on the earth as it will literally change your life!

Dr. David Herzog
David Herzog Ministries
Author of Glory Invasion
www.thegloryzone.org

"If living in the manifest presence of God's Glory is your ultimate desire, Pastor Georg Karl has provided a superb blueprint of how this is attainable. An excellent resource and revelatory book which I will be sharing with many of my personal and ministry friends."

Rev. Joshua Mills
New Wine International, Inc.
London, Ontario, Canada / Palm Springs, California
www.JoshuaMills.com

In his book "Journey Into Glory" my friend and author Georg Karl bares his heart with a candid view of his struggles and victories in his passionate pursuit for the Lord and His Glory. Not only is this 'every mans' story' in microcosm, but it also compels us to make it our victory as well. I am impressed and moved with the continued transparency and tenacity of both Georg and his wife Irina as they consistently march on with expectation and hope.

There is much to be gleaned from these pages for anyone who is hungering for more of God's Glory in their lives. The way may be fraught with misses and at time seeming defeat, but the key is never quit!

I've witnessed first hand their passion and unceasing zeal for the Lord and I have been blessed by their mission and ministry.

Take hold of the truth in these pages and you will save yourself a lot of wasted effort and receive keys to unlocking the mystery of God's Glory for your own life!

Bruce D Allen
Still Waters International Ministries
PO Box 1001
Chewelah, WA 99109

"One is tempted to say at long last! In our latitudes, the glory theology has flashed on the horizon like summer lightening for a long time. Now German-born Pastor Georg Karl presents a comprehensive, systematic revision of the subject. Without coming to hasty or unilateral conclusions, the author unfurls a biblically sound overall picture of the habitat of God's Glory, which has been originally intended for us. Plausible, stirring and liberating! Miracles and manifestations are no longer simply headlines but an integral part of an all-encompassing truth which includes the Body of Christ globally. As a reformed theologian I can recommend it wholeheartedly.

Geri Keller, reformed pastor and
founder of the Foundation Schleife/Switzerland

"And we all, who with unveiled faces all reflect the Lord's Glory, are being transformed into his likeness with ever- increasing Glory, which comes from the Lord, who is the Spirit." (2 Cor. 3:18 NIV)

Georg and Irina are two followers of Jesus who truly believe the Word of God, take it seriously and walk in it, and experience that God keeps His word.

Their ministry is a blessing in the Kingdom of God and a joy for the Lord and His children on earth.

May their ministry find a much greater favor with God and the people and open the eyes of the hearts of the children of God for the width, breadth, height and depth of the love of God.

This book will open the readers' eyes to the true heart of God and His Glory which God longs to reveal to His children."

Maria L. Prean
Leader of "Vision for Africa" (Uganda), co-founder of "Life in Jesus Christ" Mission (Austria), conference speaker and author of many books

DEDICATION

I dedicate this book to my mother Helga Karl who is already eternally in the Glory. It was through her that I heard for the first time as a small child that God is my father.

Many years later the fight for her life triggered a major impact towards a new dimension of Glory and God's miracle power in my life, even though the fight was eventually lost.

"Very truly I tell you, unless a kernel of wheat falls to the ground and dies, it remains only a single seed. But if it dies, it produces many seeds."
John 12:24 (NIV)

Published by Georg Karl.

Originally published in German by Grain-Press Verlag GmbH, Marienburger Straße 3, D-71665 Vaihingen/Enz
German Copyright © 2015 by Grain-Press
Original title: Reise in die Herrlichkeit

ISBN-10: 1546918159

ISBN-13: 978-1546918158

Contents

Introduction 13

Part I

My personal journey into the Glory 17
1. The start of the journey... 19
2. Divine appointments 25
3. Further sign posts on the journey 31
4. The path becomes clearer 37
5. The Glory manifests 43

Part II

Essence and relevance of the Glory 47
6. Kabod and Doxa 49
7. The original environment of Glory 53
8. The loss of the Glory and the era of the old covenant............ 57
9. The full gospel 63
10. How the full gospel affects us 71
11. A new creation 81
12. Identifying with the glorified Christ and reigning in the spirit 91
13. From the Glory to the harvest.................................... 105

Part III

Your journey into the Glory...113
14. "Already" and "Not Yet".. 115
15. Faith and hunger 119
16. The cross and the glory 123
17. "Falling into" the Glory... 127
18. Making the Glory of God the priority of your life................ 133

Part IV

The tangible and perceptible effects of living in the Glory................137
19. Coming alive again in the Glory.. 139
20. Inward and outward transformation through the Glory of God 147
21. Signs and wonders.. 171
22. The Glory of God and the dimension of time 213

Part V

An army is rising..233
23. The spirit of sonship and the army of the Lord 235
24. Authority and Glory... 241
25. A word of wisdom 253
26. In conclusion 265

INTRODUCTION

For the earth will be filled with the knowledge of the glory of the Lord as the waters cover the sea.
(Habakkuk 2:14)

This prophecy given through Habakkuk is about to be fulfilled! While darkness and confusion is rising in the world, God is about to confront this darkness with an ultimate visitation of His Love and His Glory as the world and also the church has never seen before.

In Isaiah 6:3 the seraphim proclaimed: *"The whole earth is filled with his glory!"* And over one hundred years later Habakkuk prophesied the appearance of this Glory in all the earth towards the conclusion of the end times. He is here talking about a manifestation which leads people and all of creation to the realization that the Glory of God is not only a theological concept but a living reality. *For the earth will be filled with the knowledge of the glory of the Lord as the waters cover the sea.* (Habakkuk 2:14)

"Knowledge" or "discernment" in a Biblical concept is much more than just "seeing", "recognizing" or "identifying" something from afar. It is not even primarily something to do with our physical eyes.

"Knowledge", in the sense of "discernment", is a deep inner awareness of the heart, a spiritual perception, a personal experience and sensation imprinting itself deep into the human spirit, thus capturing us for all eternity.

13

Habakkuk is primarily talking about spiritual senses opening up, of perceptive eyes and ears of the heart (Ephesians 1:8). But God will, in His infinite Love, also open up our spiritual senses through visible and verifiable manifestations. He knows: *"Unless you people see signs and wonders…you will never believe."* (John 4:48).

Paul's prayer in Ephesians 1:17-19 is presently coming to pass more and more: *…that the God of our Lord Jesus Christ, the glorious Father, may give you the Spirit of wisdom and revelation, so that you may know him better. I pray that the eyes of your heart may be enlightened in order that you may know the hope to which he has called you, the riches of his glorious inheritance in his holy people, and his incomparably great power for us who believe.*

A completely new move of God and His Spirit is rising on the spiritual horizon. His Glory is beginning to manifest in new ways, accompanied by unusual signs and wonders and powerful deeds, visible, tangible and verifiable.

I believe, when the Body of Christ in this age takes hold of what God is offering, we have the best chances to be the last generation of Christians here on this earth before Jesus returns: *"Heaven must receive him until the time comes for God to restore everything, as he promised long ago through his holy prophets"* (Acts 3:21).

God has begun to work worldwide in astonishing ways. Everywhere, forerunners and pioneers of this God-inspired Glory movement are rising up. Whole churches, centers and ministries are becoming high beacons of His manifest Glory here on earth, even in my home nation of Germany!

This last statement might sound quite unusual to some of our readers but for a long time we Germans were so used to only hearing and being inspired by mighty movements of God in other countries, thinking of our own nation as being a "spiritually undeveloped country".

However, this way of thinking is changing and becoming less and less true…

Right now in the German speaking nations more and more sons and daughters of God in Christ are rising up. They are letting themselves be equipped by the Holy Spirit and are being led deep into the heart of God. They are taking God up on His prophetic words and are starting to experience the manifested Glory of God personally, accompanied by all kinds of signs and wonders in the same manner as we hear about them happening in other nations. This is a sign and a wonder of itself and testifies of the intensification and acceleration of things in the Spirit worldwide in this hour of history.

The Body of Christ is a globally corporate body crossing national, cultural and generational borders. In times of worldwide media networking with resulting economic and political globalization, the move of God, in and through His Body, can no longer be viewed as being isolated events connected with only individual nations or cultures.

If something in this world is "global", it is surely His Glory!

I write this book as a German "in the natural", but at the same time as a "citizen of Heaven" and as a member of the worldwide Body of Christ, a member especially of the Body who has the goal of rising up in Glory, answering the prophetic call of God for these times, striving towards the visualization and appearance of His promises:

"Your kingdom come, your will be done, on earth as it is in heaven." (Matthew 6:10)

Now is the time! This is the finest hour of the Body of Christ, the hour of the revelation of His sons and daughters (Romans 8:19). The "glory generation" is rising!

And so I would not want to live at any other time than this...

Part I

My personal journey

into the Glory

1

THE START OF THE JOURNEY

"Father, if you really exist then come into my life and help me!" This cry, coming from the bottom of my heart during a night at the end of December 1987, would completely change my whole life.

Many years before, when I was a little boy, my mother told my sister and me about God – a God that we could call "Father". My parents were regular Lutheran Church goers, my father was on the parish council and I went with my sister to Sunday School where we heard Bible stories.

When I was 12 years old, I even gave my life to Jesus during a children's church camp which, however, did not have a long-lasting effect...

Since then, I had already left this God completely behind for some years because everything that had to do with Him seemed contradictory, the stories in the Bible were so childish and I found philosophical explan ations of the world and human life far more attractive.

I was proud of my well educated intellect which I believed was most suitable to positively change me and the world.

However, during 1987 I had come to the end of this road. To begin with I had to painfully acknowledge that my intellect was unable to find effective solutions to my various inner conflicts.

The misery inside of me grew and I began to realize that my intelligence was far too superficial to really understand the real depth of human life, let alone it succeeding. Suddenly I was aware that my thinking was crippling my personality!

At first I buried myself in psychoanalysis and soon knew all about the roots and causes of mental and emotional problems. However, I was unable to find a solution to just one of my problems.

A few New Age books were supposed to open my mind and this led me into a further (short) phase of new levels of consciousness but, at the same time, my inner misery became even more overwhelming.

Nothing seemed to help the deep cry of my soul and spirit, nothing brought relief.

I even had thoughts to just bring this meaningless existence to an end.

One day at a train station I saw a woman deeply marked by drug- addiction. It was evident that she would soon die at an early age. As she looked at me with empty and lost eyes, revelation flashed through me exposing the fact that I too, like this woman, was at an end of my rope, although no one could see it looking at me.

Shortly after, and just a few weeks before the night in 1987 I had a dream. I dreamt that I was on a high mountain surrounded by layers of dark gloomy, morbid colors.

Everything around me was forlorn with swirls of darkness, a deep chasm. I stood on this mountain completely alone and stared into the gloominess around me. My soul was torn apart and I knew that it was already a part of this darkness. The whole atmosphere was charged with total despair.

Suddenly in the dream I screamed out from my inner being with all my might into the night, "God, where are You?" and I woke up.

That dream was on my mind for quite a few days and I was very bewildered because, until then, I hadn't thought about God as a person, and I had not spoken to anyone about Him.

I did not have any contact to Christian circles – the whole world of "religion" was beyond my horizon.

Until that night a few weeks later...

I was awake lying on my bed and a horrible inner anguish tormented me – it was so intense that for weeks I had had weird pains all over my body. I knew that I was at breaking point and couldn't live like this any longer, and deep inside I was searching to grab at any kind of help – but there was none.

I felt that I'd tried all solutions that the world had to offer me and I had absolutely no trust left in anyone. Life was meaningless, full of anguish and without hope.

So, just end it?

Suddenly, quite unexpectedly (God obviously loves to show up spontaneously!), out of the innermost part of my being I had a long forgotten glimpse from my childhood – a recollection of a God that I could call Father, the God whom my mother had told me about.

Somehow, from this small thought a warmth started spreading, a sort of gentle anticipation that if there was a way out of my predicament then it must be together with this Father God. A new cry had developed in me, "Father, if you are for real then come into my life and help me!"

Silence remained, there was no visitation and I still had the pain in my body but I fell asleep feeling certain that something had significantly changed. When I woke up the next morning with a long forgotten feeling of peace, I knew that I had found the right way, and that I would, for the rest of my life, follow no other way than that of getting to know this Father God...

I did not have much of a clue about this Christian faith, and also did not know a lot about the Bible but I started a journey driven by the conscious cry in my heart for this God that I could call Father.

And thus His Spirit started to lead me without my being aware of it...

Because I'd been confirmed in the Lutheran Church I began to read books from that Christian denomination.

Almost day and night my inner being held fast to the only prayer I knew by heart: The Lord's Prayer, which starts off speaking to this Father from whom came the warmth that I had felt. I must have prayed it inwardly at least a thousand times.

Later I broadened my "prayer life" with Psalm 23.

Soon I consciously experienced an answer to prayer for the first time, and shortly after also God's personal guidance: In my search for a position with an alternative civilian service [1] I had an appointment with a minister of a Lutheran parish. While I was waiting in the outer office for the interview, my eyes fell on a Bible verse in the church newsletter on display, And he said: *Truly I tell you, unless you change and become like little children, you will never enter the kingdom of heaven.* (Matthew 18:3)

This verse gripped my attention immediately (and has been with me constantly ever since), and I knew I wanted to work there.

I got the job and over the next months I learned lots of new things about the Christian faith, with a liberal Lutheran touch. Day and night I was yearning hungrily to find out more about God and His direction for my life.

I still did not know which direction my life should take and decided to go to China for six months to teach German at a university there, which was made possible through one of my father's contacts. Afterwards, still without clarity as to which course my life should take, I went to university in Tuebingen to study history, politics and sinology (Chinese).

I joined a Bible group and for the first time in my life got to know people who talked with God loudly and freely, which fascinated me and eventually led me to a spiritual breakthrough.

I also came into contact with people who were preparing to become ministers by studying theology. This was a career that I at the time could not imagine at all.

However, one afternoon I sat there pouring over my historiographical books and felt within me a strong desire for clarity as to which road in life I should take.

My heart reached out to God and suddenly it was as though scales had fallen from my eyes, and everything around me seemed to become lighter. I knew then that my whole life, including my career, must only have something to do

---

[1] In Germany between 1956 and 2011 when men reached a certain age they were called into the army for a period of 1 year. They could apply to do a civilian job instead of military training, e.g. became male nurses in hospitals, or workers for the church etc.

with God! I was being called into full-time ministry (at the time I wasn't familiar with this term).

A few days later I started learning Greek and at the beginning of the following term, I started studying Lutheran theology. At that time I couldn't imagine another way to prepare myself for full-time ministry.

Even during my theological studies the hunger for God the Father did not leave me. Through the Lutheran theology I understood the teaching that justification comes by grace only as a free gift of God's through faith, and this resulted in a huge inner release.

I got to know all kinds of Christian groups, denominations (from Catholic to free churches) and absorbed everything that came my way.

In a pietistic (evangelical) type home cell group I perceived the significance of the personal Lordship of Jesus Christ over my life and I became "officially" born-again.

My personal relationship to God through Jesus became continually more intensive, deeper and richer. A student friend of mine suggested the so-called "charismatic circles" and my hunger drove me forward as I still wasn't sure of my destination.

2

DIVINE APPOINTMENTS

In the previous chapter, you read that during the first years of my walk with God there were several important milestones that, depending on the theological viewpoint, can be seen as a "conversion".

Without a doubt, the first 4 1⁄2 years after that night in December 1987 were especially instrumental in my intensive personal quest for God, and the seeking after as to where I stand in His plan. According to my experience, both of these always belong together:

God has a wonderful and perfect plan for every single person and the deeper we get to know Him as a Person, the deeper we are able to discern His plan for our lives!

However, this plan can only evolve in fellowship with others who have also been implanted with a similar "DNA" by God.

The more we advance in the knowledge of God, the more we recognize those that God has put us together with.

It comes from God above, but it unfolds here on earth in us and amongst us.

With this background I can say that I still hadn't found my calling from God (or my place in His Body) until the divine encounter in 1992 – and after that I still needed a number of years to actually draw the right and lasting conclusions from these encounters.

It began with a man that God sent to the university in Tuebingen. He had been invited by one of the professors who, although an atheist, wanted us to have constructive teaching from a "man in the field" in order to confront his students with another point of view. This man was a preacher from Malaysia. I immediately felt (spiritually speaking) that he was from another world and he spoke in a way that I had never experienced in Christian circles before.

I attended the "lecture" which turned out to be a sermon. He told us about unusual miracles and supernatural experiences which clearly came from a childlike faith in God!

When he was finished I knew this man had exactly what I wanted!

That night I went to a tent meeting where this man was preaching and witnessed an atmosphere in which not only miracles took place, but it seemed like heaven filled the tent. I myself experienced a healing which was made known through a word of knowledge.

I went up front to the altar and just immersed myself in this dimension of Glory, and found myself suddenly singing in a foreign language! (At this point in time I was of the opinion that I was already filled with the Holy Spirit and that talking in tongues wasn't necessary – however, God obviously thought differently!)

After this particular night, and the subsequent evenings in this tent, I knew deep within me, even if I wasn't conscious of it, that this is what I wanted. I wanted to live in an atmosphere like this and wanted to serve God like that!

Today, I know that the atmosphere in these meetings was the result of the manifestation of the Glory of God (heaven on earth) although I didn't know these terms then.

HOW DO YOU ACTUALLY RECOGNIZE THE GLORY OF GOD?

The question arises: How do you actually recognize the manifestation of the Glory of God? How does one perceive whether the Glory of God has manifested in a church service or not?

This question cannot be answered satisfactorily with intellect.

One thing is for certain – when the atmosphere in a room is charged with the Glory of God, it is recognized immediately by the hungry spirit of a person as being the answer to the deep yearning in one's inner self!

The person feels intuitively that this is what he has always searched for and from this moment on he is ruined for anything less!

The Glory of God can be recognized through the *effect* of manifested signs and wonders, or of people being deeply touched, profoundly changed, or their hearts being set on fire. However, alone by faith, miracles can also take place without any sort of perceptible manifestation of the Glory of God, or through the gift of healing received from God.

When it comes to a change of heart it is also difficult to draw explicit conclusions – it depends on the depth of change as well as the direction it takes, and who could really assess it from the outside? A secular motivational speaker can also fire up his listeners without it having anything to do with God.

Ultimately, we can summarize that the Glory of God and His presence can only be perceived and taken in from spirit to Spirit. *"Deep calls to deep"* (Psalm 42:7). "Babes in Christ" are often not conscious of this happening but those with trained spiritual senses (Hebrews 5:14) become more and more conscious of it.

When you have really experienced the Glory of God and have opened up your spirit to the Spirit of Glory then you are "ruined" for anything less than this. Even without being aware of it, you always hunger deep down for the manifestation of God's presence.

The Glory of God is perceived from "spirit to Spirit" – from a person's hungering spirit to the Spirit of God!

If you don't continually make a conscious decision for this lifestyle and purpose of life, and the adversary manages for a longer period of time to keep you away from God's Glory, then a phase of hardship, trials and tribulations will come your way until you, through spiritual insight, make a mature lifetime decision to return to God's glory!

The decision will probably look something like this: "I have been born for the Glory and I live for it. I put everything aside to have it and make this yearning for the Glory in me my lifestyle. For the rest of my life no one and nothing shall ever again lead me away from focusing on this!

More of you Lord – more of your Glory[2]!"

I believe that now is the time that God will raise and bring together an "army" of committed people who are no longer prepared to compromise when it comes to the Glory of God. This doesn't mean that this army won't be willing to learn, and to grow in revelation and knowledge, but when it's about this aspect – the pursuance of the supernatural presence of God, and manifest Glory, then it is without compromise: no circumstance, barrier, withdrawal of people's approval, not even if it comes from other Christians, no persecution, slander or defamation of any kind or from whatever source will prevent us from standing for God's Glory, hungering for the manifestation of His presence and to have faith in it wherever we are!

...However, in 1992 I had unfortunately not yet progressed that far:

The vital difference between the tent meeting in Tuebingen to any of the other Christian meetings wasn't clear to me at that time. I therefore tried out various things in the field of Christianity and, even though everything was biblically based, I became aware that I received no real fulfillment, no direction and peace. This left me empty and confused and my hunger for the real thing became desperate!

During the fall of 1992 I was invited to a church service in Stuttgart. At the time there were many rumors and stories circulating amongst the theologians at the university about this church and they weren't exactly positive! Nonetheless, something pulled at me to go.

This was again a divine appointment. Right from the beginning the atmosphere was electrified. When the preacher began to speak I was aware that he was obviously under a heavenly, supernatural current.

---

[2] Further explanations and biblical definitions about the nature of the Glory of God can be found in Part II, Chapters 6 and 7

The whole hall was charged with an indescribably awesome prickling! And then a word of knowledge hit me straight in my heart.

I will never forget this tingling presence of God at this church service – it was yet another encounter with the Glory of God!

Although this church was far from Tuebingen, I visited the services regularly and the Glory that was set free there, without my noticing, increasingly accompanied and guided me.

A few months later, God spoke to me personally with regard to my future assignment in His kingdom. The first stage was that I go to Bible School parallel to my studies and then to establish a church in the Tuebingen/Reutlingen area. In a dream this scenario was shown to me 1 1/2 years before it actually happened!

In this dream I also saw my future wife Irina whom I had got to know at a charismatic revival group of theology students. At the time I was unaware of the significance she would have in my life.

A short time later this dream was confirmed in my heart by a prophetic word and by God speaking to me personally.

After both completing bible school, Irina and I got married in July 1994. We then began the church planting process.

In summer 1995 while we were painting walls in our new church rooms and I was working by myself, the Holy Spirit spoke to me, *"I will set my glory down in this place!"*

At this point of time I still did not have a real understanding as to what the Glory of God is. However, already being familiar with Bible talk at the time this sentence had power! At any rate, after hearing this word, I figured our project of establishing a church would be a great success...

3

FURTHER SIGN POSTS ON THE

JOURNEY

At first our church project was a real success. Nearly every Sunday people gave their life to Christ and quite a few amazing healings and miracles happened. The congregation grew quickly and within a year we already had 100 members.

Over New Year 1996/97 Irina and I went to the Erzgebirge (mountain range between Germany and the Czech Republic) for a few days to spend quality time with God and to ask for guidance with regard to the coming year.

During this time, God spoke very clearly to me. He said, "It cannot go on like this!"

I had the impression that although our church was successful something important was missing. I did not know what it was but because God spoke to me I knew I should ask Him for a new move of His Spirit.

It became clear to me that we had brought people into our church through our *own* efforts, and that we would only hold them with our *own* strength if we did not lay a solid foundation of God's supernatural strength and effectiveness.

I did not realize at the time that we had subconsciously created a church with an atmosphere of religious pressure, works, legalism and self-ambition, instead of living in and out of an atmosphere of God's Glory and His presence.

Our main goal was to have a quick-growing church instead of having the living person of God and His supernatural Glory dwelling in our midst!

Please don't get me wrong, God does want our churches to grow and we should have a vision for that, but what is more important to Him is the spiritual environment in which this church can grow. Is it a supernatural environment of the Glory of God, or is it a humanly Christian, i.e. ultimately a "religious" environment?

I had not learnt yet to interpret the information which God had given me during the previous years when He told me *"My Glory is your calling, it's your life – in My Glory and within My manifested presence you'll live and flourish – outside of it you'll wither and die."* (See Deuteronomy 30:19-20!)

I have now learnt that keeping the Glory of God in our midst as the Body of Christ is one of the most difficult challenges, but by far the most rewarding and satisfying!

At any rate, for me there is absolutely no alternative – it is the only thing on earth that is really worth living for!

What is the benefit of having the recognition of people just so that I am "left in peace" by the devil and, by doing so, I have to give up the greatest prize – His Glory and the manifestation of Him personally!?

During those days at the turn of the year, it became very clear to me that in order to come into my calling from God I would need a new, deeper understanding of God in my life and that was what I needed to stretch out for!

Back then, just being 27 years old, wisdom and patience were not exactly great characteristics of mine (to put it lightly), and when I got back, I immediately shared my new and intensified hunger for God with the whole church.

A few weeks later we also heard about a powerful spiritual awakening in the USA and so we were unable to contain ourselves. As soon as we could, we got the videos of this revival (in those days CDs and MP3's did not yet exist). I once again felt this electrified atmosphere in the services there which had gripped me a few years earlier!

I immediately got on this bandwagon with flying flags, even though the theological (more like Arminianism[3]) orientation of this movement in America had a totally different emphasis to what I was familiar with.

It wasn't the theological teaching that drew me but just being able to feel the mighty presence of God and His Glory in those meetings which gave me this deep inner urge, "You have to have this in your church!"

As I have said before, at the time I did not have the understanding of this glory and its character. In my immaturity I tried to copy this USA revival by preaching the same messages and reckoned that within a short span of time a similar mighty breakthrough would happen with us. We did indeed have a few powerful and glory filled services but, due to my inexperience and ignorance, upheavals and painful divisions in the church followed. Although I desired it so much I wasn't capable to hold the manifestation and glory in the church for more than 2 to 3 weeks!

Watching recordings of the revival in the USA (Irina and I travelled there twice to experience it) had great impact on me and catapulted me to a high level of power and glory but I couldn't cope with the subsequent tension that resulted amongst some of the congregation because of it. I had to continually put up with feeling a failure caused by the reaction of the people which hurt and I eventually, at times, fell into a deep depression. I knew that I had touched and embraced a spiritual substance which belonged to my calling and not for anything did I want to lose sight of my goal. However, there were so many things in my soul that got in the way.

The lack of spiritual understanding did the rest so that in the following years my soul went through many phases of frustration which gave way to times of holy revolt and uprise, which can maybe be compared with Samson who, after the loss of his eyesight, could only make a last desperate effort in the power of God...

In 1998 we came in touch with a new wave of how God can work. Gold dust, precious stones and even heavenly manna manifested in our midst!

---

[3] A theological school of thought that sharply contradicts Calvinism especially to do with the cooperation and contribution of man for his salvation.

This again was a short period where this extraordinary substance that today I can identify and discern as being the Glory of God manifested in our midst before everything yet again collapsed as I wasn't able to maintain my focus on it because of the turbulent circumstances around me. This definitely also had to do with my lack of good teaching about living life in the Spirit and the Glory. In view of all the outward circumstances and problems I did not know what to concentrate on. (I would have found the answer in 2 Corinthians 3:18![4])

Looking back, one can define those years as being the years in the fiery furnace or the desert years, and I can only marvel over the grace of God who didn't allow our church to disappear off the face of the earth and bring our ministry to a premature end!

I eventually came to the conclusion that a ministry that didn't move in the supernatural sphere would be more desirable because the supernatural was connected with so many attacks and, with the help of various concepts, I tried to stabilize the church on a lower spiritual level. Naturally at the time I would never have looked at it like that!

But in truth I had long since been "ruined" for any spiritually lower level than I had already experienced, and for what God had called me for.

I endeavored to find good teaching for our church, trained the church members in the spiritual gifts, invited prophets, evangelists, teachers and apostles to serve us, organized conferences and strove interdenominationally for the unity of the Body of Christ.

Inwardly I kept running out of steam. It didn't matter how hard I tried, there was no resounding success.

After about 7 years, I was on the verge of a nervous breakdown. I continually felt as though I was wedged in a vice and unable to move in any direction or to free myself. I didn't know how long I would be able to stick it out and without doubt I wouldn't have made it if Jesus hadn't carried me through!

---

[4] And we all, who with unveiled faces contemplate the Lord's Glory, are being transformed into his image with ever-increasing Glory, which comes from the Lord, who is the Spirit.

When I had hit rock bottom, God gave me a word at the end of 2003 in a communion service in the Berlin Protestant Cathedral: *"But I have prayed for you, that your faith may not fail."* (Luke 22:32)

I cried and from that moment on I knew deep down more than ever before that, completely outside of my own strength and ability, I was being carried and held by His endless grace.

A short while later, at the beginning of 2004, we heard of a new movement of God in Germany and at the first meeting that we visited, Irina and I felt once again, for the first time in years, this heavenly substance that we had experienced in America and also in Tuebingen and Stuttgart in 1992!

We felt revived and were brought in touch with the thread of our calling once again.

After a while, with many extremely positive experiences and landmark revelations giving us direction, we came to the conclusion that there are always two sides that you can fall from a horse:

With regard to a life in the Glory of God there is, on the one hand, the temptation to get away from the pressure the devil builds up against the manifestation of the Glory so that one tries to maneuver the Glory of God in such a way that it doesn't offend the people's flesh, especially the "religious spirit". You can also describe this temptation as being "people-pleasing".

Paying too much attention to your "good reputation" in the long term disqualifies you from becoming a carrier of God's manifested Glory!

The opposite temptation is to try and make sure not to come under any "(religious) spirits", and to withdraw completely from those various parts of the Body of Christ who tend to question and eye you critically, and through whom you may also come under the fire of "religious spirits" from time to time.

The latter extreme leads to a heart-attitude that doesn't want to be corrected, to pride and spiritual isolation from the Body of Christ and then from Jesus, the head of the Body Himself. This consequently leads to a spiritual imbalance which, in turn, makes it impossible for the Glory of God to be with us and manifest in our midst!

When I began to see these truths more and more clearly in 2008/09 it led me to search even more intensely for personal guidance from God, and for answers to my many questions. A number of insights in this book deal with what He, in His mercy, showed me.

4

THE PATH BECOMES CLEARER

Since my turning to God in December 1987, I have never consciously yearned for anything else in my life than to know and do the will of God, my Father.

It was therefore only natural that with this new crisis I knew that only the pursuit of Jesus Christ as a person, and thus also the Father, together with following the revelation of His word in the Bible closely, would lead me to a deeper perception of His will.

The first Bible verse that the Holy Spirit gave me anew was Luke 4:18-19:

The Spirit of the Lord is on me, because he has anointed me to proclaim good news to the poor. He has sent me to proclaim freedom for the prisoners and recovery of sight for the blind, to set the oppressed free, to proclaim the year of the Lord's favor.

More than ever before, I became deeply aware that if I wanted to maintain the course in my life towards God's calling, then the purpose of the anointing on Jesus – and on us – must have top priority.

God wouldn't rest permanently on a person with His glory and favor if that person hadn't made one of God's most important desires his own, and that desire is the harvest!

When he saw the crowds, he had compassion on them, because they were harassed and helpless, like sheep without a shepherd. Then he said to his disciples, "The harvest is plentiful but the workers are few. Ask the Lord of the harvest, therefore, to send out workers into his harvest field." (Matthew 9:36-38)

We must be moved by that which moves God's heart and then His Spirit will also move on our behalf!

Focusing on the harvest – God's heart for the lost –keeps us on the right course spiritually!

Since fall 2006, we have held evangelistic healing services in our church every month. They have definitely helped to keep our focus on carrying out God's Great Commission.

For a long time, I had asked God if I was really qualified for such a job. One afternoon, while driving, the Holy Spirit suddenly spoke very clearly to my heart, *He who heals the sick lives in you!* With that, I knew I was qualified by Jesus Himself in me!

Many Christians are waiting for a special supernatural manifestation or for a specific life changing experience as confirmation that God has really called them to heal or be used for miracles! But really the bottom line is that alone Christ in us is already a fully sufficient qualification!

In 2008/09, whilst specifically stretching out for more of God's direction for my life and our ministry, the Holy Spirit again pointed out to me that the great harvest could only be carried out effectively within the realms of the supernatural with signs and wonders following!

This can be seen very clearly in the person and the ministry of Jesus Christ here on earth, and also in the Bible-reports about His followers in Acts, and in the New Testament epistles.

On the one hand, the Word of God gives us crucial guidelines how not to revert to legalistic and, therefore, dead activities while, on the other hand, also not falling into a pseudo spiritual fanaticism with destructive deceptions. The key is to focus our lives and ministry on carrying out the assignment of the Kingdom in the supernatural power of God!

The devil would love to take the supernatural "crowning" of our lives and ministries. Over the years I have intensively experienced his wheelings and dealings– because he knows that if we come into a supernatural life it will make us to what Christians really should be – effective world-changers!

The Great Commission of GOD can only be effectively carried out in the supernatural!

We need to make the decision once and for all not to do the devil a favor and allow ourselves to be distracted from the actual core of being a Christian.

A necessary prerequisite for this is described in Proverbs 3:5-6:

Trust in the Lord with all your heart and lean not on your own understanding; in all your ways submit to him, and he will make your paths straight.

God already gave me this verse when I was baptized as a believer in 1993.

In 2012 God once again spoke personally to me "I will make you – the formerly intellectual – to be a sign for the supernatural power of God and life in the Spirit. Through this I am making you to be a sign showing the way that I wish to lead the Body of Christ – away from intellect and into trusting the Spirit of God!"

From the very beginning (read the Bible!), the essence of Christianity is 100 % supernatural and nothing has changed since then –the supernatural is even more important and vital today than in any previous generation – because Jesus is coming soon!

A fundamental reshaping is about to happen in the "Country of Poets and Thinkers"[5] and for its Christian "landscape"!

More and more Christians are becoming aware that, in the long run, we need to get back into the Word of God, the recorded foundations of the Body of Christ, e.g. 1 Corinthians 2:5 and 4:20, in order to actually fulfill our calling:

---

[5] This is a "title" often given to Germany as a nation, but it certainly also applies to most of the western world.

The effectively demonstrated supernatural power of God! For the kingdom of God is not a matter of talk but of power...

In order for us to have this power in our lives permanently, we need to make a clear and profound decision for precisely this way, because, as said before, the devil will try – whether it's through problems and circumstances or through natural, fleshly and for our outer man apparently more pleasant alternatives – to distract our focus.

As mentioned before I experienced this for years but the breakthrough from my own "trials and tribulations" came when I clearly cottoned on to the ins and outs of it and was then able to make my decision!

AN UNEXPECTED SHOCK

At the end of the year 2009 another painful shock occurred in my (natural) family which also accelerated my personal journey. My mother was told by the doctors that the cancer she had was beyond treatment, and that she only had a limited period of time to live.

Irina and I, together with my parents, decided we would trust God to heal her supernaturally through His Word.

Shortly after we had committed ourselves to this fight for life and death, I had an impulse from the Holy Spirit to intensify my reaching out for a real breakthrough in miracle healing in my ministry. God also reminded me of videos that we had watched and recorded on television of a revival that was broadcast on a Christian channel in 2008.

In these meetings there wasn't only a powerful healing and miracle anointing but also an indescribable manifestation of the presence of God over a period of many weeks. For nights-on-end we sat in front of the TV as though spellbound and drank in this amazing freshness!

At the beginning of 2010 I took these videos from the shelf again and I absorbed this spiritual substance with a whole new hunger and determination. During this time, I reached out for a new dimension of the healing and miracle power of God and studied and proclaimed His Word pertaining to this.

This went on for quite a few months until a decisive breakthrough happened in July 2010. Almost overnight a completely new dimension of the Glory and miracle power of God showed up in our church – extraordinary creative miracles happened both in our church services as well as on the street, and in the everyday lives of our church members. An altogether new presence of God began to settle on our meetings.

I lay under the power and Glory of God at the end of one of our church services in September 2010 and God spoke to me, *"This glory that is now here will substantially change everything!"*

5

THE GLORY MANIFESTS

And that is just what happened!

On our journey into the Glory, God had guided us right up to the entrance of our promised land and it became increasingly clear to me that I would never want to, or be able to, leave this land of my calling – but rather that my journey would lead me ever deeper into this land!

Despite our faith and intensive prayers for my mother, she succumbed to cancer in November and went before us into the untainted Glory of the Lord. At the same time, extraordinary miracles and healings happened in our ministry (also from cancer)! Her death was thus not only extremely painful for me personally but also seemingly a defeat of our faith in the complete victory of Jesus Christ over sickness as part of His atonement.

At the same time, I knew immediately that this experience should in no way discourage me. As a matter of fact, this tragedy was unable to keep me from my further progress and reaching out toward even more of His miracle working and manifest glory in my life and in our ministry.

Yes, this experience ultimately strengthened my determination!

God gave me a wonderful confirmation when He said to me, "The death of your mother is like a seed for this ministry of healing and miracles and it will become a symbol of God's heart for this world. *"Very truly I tell you, unless a kernel of wheat falls to the ground and dies, it remains only a single seed. But if it dies, it produces many seeds.* " John 12:24 (NIV)

Thus it became apparent that after this sad death, my obligation towards living in the glory, including signs and wonders from God's perspective, had become more urgent.

I am eternally grateful to God for the way He molded my heart during these particularly significant years of formation. It was a process through numerous difficulties which, from a human point of view, were often insurmountable. During that process He gave me many revelations, personal supernatural encounters and guidance that led me to important decisions for my life so that the last remnants of uncertainty to do with God's calling of living in His Glory fell away. I was increasingly able to see the whole picture of His Divine plan – not only for my life – but also for the Body of Jesus Christ as a whole in the end times!

There are also many of God's vessels who are presently active worldwide in the Body of Christ to whom I owe very important impulses – it would become a very long list if I mentioned them all!

I had stepped into a completely new land as I saw things come together more and more and thereby also saw the reasons for the times spent "in the desert" (which I hope many readers of this book won't have to go through[6]). It is a land of freedom and abundance, deep inner peace and being certain that I was at last on my way to my calling in God!

I experienced, and am still experiencing, that which Paul mentions in Romans 8:21 (KJV) *"the glorious liberty of the children of God"*. I desire nothing more than that as many sons and daughters of God as possible will get

---

[6] Even though I do know that to a certain extent such times are necessary to bring about maturity – see Romans 8:28 *And we know that all things work together for good to them that love God, to them who are the called according to his purpose* (KJV), and Romans 5:3-5 *Not only so, but we also glory in our sufferings, because we know that suffering produces perseverance; perseverance, character; and character, hope.And hope does not put us to shame, because God's love has been poured out into our hearts through the Holy Spirit, who has been given to us.* It's not for nothing that Paul writes in 2 Corinthians 12:12 about the characteristics of the apostle: *I **persevered** in demonstrating among you the marks of a true apostle, including signs, wonders and miracles!!*

to know and walk on this path of Glory which God, in His infinite grace and love, intended for us as children of the new covenant.

Since 2010 we have personally, and also in our church, moved in a "bubble of glory" that frequently completely shielded us from any external pressure to compromise in relation to our clear-cut focus on Jesus Christ as our Lord and Head, the revelation of the Word in the Bible, as well as our supernatural calling in Christ and His Glory!

At the exact right time and right moment (never too early and never too late) God confirmed His Word through amazing signs and wonders and gave us the favor and the open doors that we needed in order to continue on His way.

With growing clarity and determination we continue to proceed on this path accompanied by an ever increasing glory and thickness of His presence whereby we no longer follow after signs and wonders because they now follow us (see Mark 16:17)!

I am continually delighted to see how people are supernaturally transformed by the Glory of God – in body, soul and spirit – the way they blossom by breathing in heaven's air. It is exciting how the Holy Ghost calls together and raises up an ever-increasing powerful troop of pioneers on this planet in His power that is always fresh and who then, actively and effectively, bring in the harvest for God!

People are transformed in God's glorious environment, they blossom and become carriers of the Glory themselves.

By studying what God is doing worldwide in the Body of Christ, and through my personal contacts with key people in the present movement of His Spirit, I am continually reassured that God has a new plan to offer the Body of Christ as a whole for these times. Being His sons and daughters, God offers us a deeper calling to be the actual dwelling place of God's Glory here on earth during the end times. Out of this Glory we will bring in the harvest, not only individually, but also collectively. The house of God is being built now and its Glory will be greater than the Glory of the former house!

"This is what the Lord Almighty says: 'In a little while I will once more shake the heavens and the earth, the sea and the dry land. I will shake all nations, and what is desired by all nations will come, and I will fill this house with glory,' says the Lord Almighty. 'The silver is mine and the gold is mine,' declares the Lord Almighty. 'The glory of this present house will be greater than the glory of the former house,' says the Lord Almighty. 'And in this place I will grant peace,' declares the Lord Almighty." Haggai 2:6-9

This book has been written to contribute towards increasingly bringing this vision into reality. To this end I strive to give God-hungry hearts good biblical foundations as well as inspiration, challenge and encouragement for a permanent life as a "temple of Glory"...

PART II
ESSENCE AND
RELEVANCE OF THE
GLORY

6

KABOD AND DOXA

People have all sorts of different ideas when they hear the word "Glory". Behind the saying "This is glorious!" people imagine feeling extremely good or happy, or being in a perfect atmosphere or place where everything is just great, and that is not far from the truth...

But the Glory that the Bible talks about is always directly connected with God!

It is the essence of His Being, the substance of all that God is. It encompasses His whole "weight" ("Kabod" is the Hebrew word for weight).

God is a Person with such a tremendous "weight" that it is impossible to confine Him in some kind of form like a human body. Rather, He is such an all-dominant Being and is continually accompanied by an awe-inspiring radiation of power and energy that there are no words to describe Him. The best word used for this is GLORY!

God's Glory cannot be separated from His Person and, likewise, His Person cannot be separated from His Glory.

Wherever God is personally manifested, His Glory is also present.

Behind the "weight", the radiance, the "cloud" – or however you wish to describe it – the Person is present!

A much weaker comparison would be that of a person who, for some reason or other, develops a special radiance. This can be the result of a position of power that they hold in the world, or it can also be a specific "charisma" or a radiance through various forms of "spirituality".

The most powerful radiance (and here the term "glorious" is absolutely justifiable) should be found in the sons and daughters of God who will be revealed in Christ (Romans 8:19-21, 1 Corinthians 2:7, Hebrews 2:10 etc.) – because the true and pure Glory of God radiates from them, which is the whole weight (Kabod) of His Son Jesus Christ in them.

The Greek word that the New Testament uses for Glory is "**Doxa**", and it unfolds the richness of its meaning even further. It means something like majesty, excellence, beauty, power, magnificence, might, honor, wealth, fullness, dignity and the royalty of a person!

Biblically speaking, all this describes God's Person, His Being, His essence and, likewise, also the essence of His resurrected Son Jesus who is sitting at His right hand. See John 1:14 *"The Word became flesh and made his dwelling among us. We have seen his glory, the glory of the one and only Son, who came from the Father, full of grace and truth."*

Wherever God is present and perceived by faith then this "Doxa" manifests!

The Glory of God is the "radiation" which surrounds His Person and which, at the same time, is the perfect expression of His Being!

When the Glory of God – He Himself – manifests in you and around you – then your spirit is imbued with a deep sense of the majesty and royalty of God. You receive an overwhelming revelation of His magnificence, might and power, or your heart simply enjoys His excellence and beauty! All of these are the discernable "side effects" of the manifestation of "God's Doxa" in our midst!

God yearns more and ever more to reveal His Glory to us and thereby also Himself.

Against this background let me share with you a few basic revelations from the Word to do with the significance of the "Glory" in God's plan for humanity.

It is very important to realize that what is presented in the following chapters isn't just intellectual knowledge. It is rather *revelation* knowledge that you must grasp with your spirit. By taking in the revelation on the level beyond reasoning, the explosive power that is contained in it will unfold.

7

THE ORIGINAL ENVIRONMENT

OF GLORY

Basically the Bible teaches that God and his son Jesus Christ are everywhere – God is omnipresent.

Therefore, the whole earth, including the entire universe and, if existent, even all the "parallel universes", are *"filled with His Glory"* (Isaiah 6:3).

However, since the fall, mankind and the rest of creation face a spiritual problem.

In the Garden of Eden, the original habitat of man, there wasn't any separation between God and His creation. Everything created, even the atmosphere, was fully penetrated by His essence and Glory.

Heaven, the invisible and immaterial dwelling place of God, was freely accessible from earth, the dwelling place of creation.

Yes, heaven and earth were actually quite naturally "neighbors".

In the description of the Garden of Eden in Genesis 2:8-14, we find that besides all the natural trees God also planted two supernatural trees/heavenly trees– the tree of life and the tree of knowledge of good and evil (verse 9).

We also read about four rivers, two of them being totally terrestrial (Euphrates and Tigris) and two others that have never existed on the earth as known to us (Pishon and Gihon) (verses 11-14).

Heaven and earth existed immediately adjacent to one another and permeated each other. They were thereby both completely engulfed in the omnipresence of God – His Glory!

You could describe it like this: The air mankind was breathing was surely the same natural air as we know it today – but it was likewise also intermingled and joined with God's heavenly Glory "air" which filled all of Eden.

This "air" enabled mankind and all the other creatures to live without sickness, feebleness, ageing, decay and death – it was the "umbilical cord" that connected them permanently to their Almighty, Everlasting Creator.

This air made Eden what it was – literally "constant pleasure" and "everlasting joy".

This glorious atmosphere was of vital importance especially to mankind, who were (and are) created as spiritual beings in God's likeness. You can look at it this way – what water is to a fish, soil to a mole and natural air to a bird – that is God's Glory for humanity in accordance with the Divine Order of creation.

Only in this habitat can humankind really fulfill its divine destiny and flourish in what God ordained for them before the foundation of the world.

Man was living in this perfect habitat in Eden – totally shielded and protected from every outside ungodly influence opposing the order of creation. Mankind was sort of enclosed in a bubble of Glory in which God, in His love, had surrounded His entire creation.

Simultaneously this 'bubble of glory' and humanity were constantly connected with heaven, that is to God and all He stands for. The life of man thus took place in Glory, from Glory and to Glory.

The fellowship of mankind with their Creator and His Glory was absolutely untroubled.

Eden was completely and utterly "heaven on earth"!

SUMMARY:

- The heavens and the terrestrial realms formed a unity in Eden

- All realms of creation were thereby enwrapped in the Glory of God

- Man permanently not only breathed natural air but also God's Glory air, which kept him in a constant state of perfection.

8

THE LOSS OF THE GLORY AND

THE ERA OF THE OLD

COVENANT

At the point of time when Adam willfully relinquished his God-given authority over creation to the devil by becoming submissive to him (Genesis 3:1-7), God had to create a separation – on the one hand from fallen man and, on the other hand, from the Glory of God. God did this to protect mankind so that they would not have to live forever as fallen creatures (see Genesis 3:22-24)![7]

Contrary to popular belief, God did not primarily banish man to punish him, but to protect him!

This banishment entailed a "curtain" that permanently divided man from Eden's "air of glory" and, at the same time, divided heaven and earth completely!

---

[77]And the Lord God said, "The man has now become like one of us, knowing good and evil. He must not be allowed to reach out his hand and take also from the tree of life and eat, and live forever." So the Lord God banished him from the Garden of Eden to work the ground from which he had been taken. After he drove the man out, he placed on the east side of the Garden of Eden cherubim and a flaming sword flashing back and forth to guard the way to the tree of life.

There is no difference between Jew and Gentile, for all (in Adam) have sinned and fall short of the glory of God (Romans 3:22-23) – the cherubim that God placed at the entrance of Eden made sure of this!

At the same time the fact described in Isaiah 6:3 that the whole of creation is still filled and soaked with His Glory remains intact.

But since the fall of man, the natural senses of the unredeemed creation are entirely veiled with an invisible "spiritual curtain", separating the earthly from the heavenly. This, as a result, also separates mankind from the perception of the Glory and life within the original "glory bubble".

The consequences of this separation from life in the "glory bubble" were very dramatic, and the further away man was from Eden the worse it got.

Step by step premature aging and death marched in (evidence of this is that the life expectancy of humankind has continually decreased as from the generation of Adam[8]).

Jealousy, which resulted in murder and manslaughter, followed (see Genesis 4 – Cain and Abel). They were the automatic outcome brought about by the separation from the unconditional safety in the love of God in the original glory bubble. From there things ceaselessly spiraled downwards…

In the time of Noah, decay and wickedness reached such dimensions that God, without further ado, attempted a new start with Noah and his children (see Genesis 6:1 to 9:17). However, this ultimately didn't really change anything – already in Genesis 9:18-27 you can read about the next act of wickedness.

---

[8]Could it perhaps be that the reason why an increase of life expectancy over the last 150 years has come about is because there are more and more sons and daughters of God on the earth and, therefore, God's Glory is increasingly released and manifested? To be more specific, could it be that the medical and technical advancement that man has been given the credit for is, in reality, the result of the "spiritual advancement" that the Body of Christ has made during this age? It is at any rate noticeable that, historically, the significant medical breakthroughs at the end of the 19th and beginning of the 20th centuries have actually occurred parallel to supernatural healing ministries popping up all over the world.
I believe that a lot more than we observe and experience outwardly in human history has spiritual reasons and, therefore its origin in the Body of Christ.

In reality, this attempt only confirmed the fact that humankind is nonviable outside of the Glory of God – resulting also in the suffering of the rest of creation entrusted to him!

There was no way left other than for God to directly and personally intervene in order to bring back access and life in the Glory to earth, so that true life could once again be made possible for humanity!

ABRAHAM

This intervention started with calling out Abraham, "the father of faith" (Romans 4:11 onwards), from his ancestral land into a land that God had chosen for him and giving him the encouragement that the blessings he would need would be available (Genesis 12:1-3).

> **After the unavoidable expulsion of man from the environment of Glory, God was left with only one choice of personal intervention in order to once again make His Glory *accessible* to creation!**

The promised land of Canaan that Abraham moved to was the first clear, natural "foreshadow" in the Old Testament for the habitat of God's Glory that was to be retaken for mankind in the New Covenant. Abraham crossed this land in all directions, and eventually became settled there with his descendants – in the same way it is destined in the New Covenant for the sons and daughters of God, in the Spirit, to become settled in the Glory!

MOSES

Hundreds of years later, Moses was to lead the children of Israel out of Egypt[9]. In the meantime, they had become a multitude and were far from their Land of Promise. At this point, for the first time, God from His side broke through the perceived curtain sovereignly which, since the fall of man, had stood immovable between mankind and the Glory of God. As a result, mankind was, for the first time, able to perceive the manifestation of the Glory of God on this fallen earth with their natural senses. It occurred in the form of a pillar

---

[9] A foreshadow of living in estrangement from the land of Glory!

of cloud by day, and a pillar of fire by night (Exodus 40:34-38). Respectively, on Mount Sinai, there was fire and a dark cloud of smoke (see Exodus 19:16-18).

This visible Glory of God led and accompanied the people of Israel during their wandering in the wilderness. We should keep in mind here that God's chosen man Moses found these manifestations totally positive, daring to fully trust them, while the rest of the people were afraid and kept their distance in fear! The awareness of sin was deeply engrained since the fall, and with it came the shame and fear of God and His Glory.

During the whole era of the Old Testament, God only revealed His Glory to a few chosen men and women whom He personally called and drew into His confidence.

Ezekiel, for example, stands out amongst them in a special way. He had many very profound experiences with the Glory of God which you can read about in Ezekiel 1-3 and Ezekiel 47. These are quite similar to John's visions in Revelations 4 and 22.

In this context, the descent ("Shekinah" in Hebrew) of the Glory of God during the dedication of the first temple by Solomon (1 Kings 8:10-11; 2 Chronicles 5:11-14) needs to be mentioned. The temple in Jerusalem thus succeeded the "tent of meeting" at the time of Moses, where the cloud of glory had regularly manifested in those days (see Exodus 33:9-11).

As the era of the Old Covenant approached the end, more prophecies were given about the future manifestation of God's Glory. Above all, as quoted before by Habakkuk in chapter 2:14 *For the earth will be filled with the knowledge of the glory of the Lord as the waters cover the sea.*

Here, for the first time the complete falling of the curtain was foretold, which, since the fall, had seemingly insurmountably separated man from the awareness of and life in God's Glory.

One of the last prophets of the Old Covenant, Haggai, saw in his prophetic vision the outcome of the fulfillment of Habakkuk's prophecy by announcing:

In a little while I will once more shake the heavens and the earth, the sea and the dry land. I will shake all nations, and what is desired by all nations will come, and I will fill this house with glory,' says the Lord Almighty... 'The glory of this present house will be greater than the glory of the former house,' says the Lord Almighty. 'And in this place I will grant peace,' declares the Lord Almighty." (Haggai 2:6-9)

SUMMARY

- After man became partakers of Satan's nature through sin, God had to expel him, together with his entrusted creation, from the environment of Glory.

- The result was the rapidly accelerating degeneration of mankind. This could only be alleviated by occasional sovereign and progressive revelations of God's Glory and this was limited only to the people of Israel.

- However, towards the end of the era of the Old Covenant, more and more prophets appeared on the scene who prophesied a future with an absolutely new dimension of the revelation of God's Glory over the whole earth.

9

THE FULL GOSPEL

In the Old Covenant, the Glory occasionally manifested discernably through the direct intervention of God. As a result, every now and then a glimpse was enabled beyond the curtain which had been erected after the fall of man. However, these were always very limited and restricted to short periods of time.

The weight of sin was too heavy for mankind, the separation from God was too drastic and therewith also from man's original habitat: *For the wages of sin is death* (Romans 6:23). Whereby "death" in this sense is nothing else than the complete separation from the environment of God's Glory.

Basically there was only one way for God to make a fundamental change to the situation – He had to Himself intervene personally in form of the unique Person of His Son.

In the Father's heart, even before the foundation of the world, Christ had already been selected as the lamb for this plan (Revelations 13:8). He had resided in the Glory of God since the beginning (John 17:5) *"When the set time had fully come"* (Galatians 4:4), it was the moment for His mission to begin. On command of the Father, Christ Himself gave up the Glory He had with the Father (Philippians 2:7), and took on the form of a "bond-servant", a human being, with the name Jesus amongst the people in the kingdom of the devil! He then carried the sins of all mankind on the cross and, through His resurrection, and with the outpouring of the Holy Spirit, overcame, once and for all, the separation of mankind from the Glory of God. The curtain is torn – without any further ado, the way is really free!

Surprisingly for some, the Bible report on the "drama of God becoming a human" also gives the following conclusive statement that whilst Jesus was on earth He did everything according to what one reads in the gospels as a man and not as God! If it were not so then the abandonment of the Glory that we can read about in Philippians 2 couldn't have taken place, and Jesus could not have accomplished complete salvation and the opening up of the curtain.

Everything that Jesus did in His ministry on earth He did as a son of man having completely given up His heavenly Glory.

He was indeed still God on earth, but was completely without any connecting benefits.

At the beginning of His earthly life the only difference between Jesus and the people of His time, besides His supernatural conception, was that He didn't give in to any kind of temptation from the devil – which means that He lived without sin (Hebrews 4:15).

Not until God sovereignly tore open the curtain to heaven over Jesus at the Jordan (Mark 1:10-11), and the Holy Spirit, as a direct connection to the Father, descended on Him, was Jesus empowered for His supernatural ministry.

With the anointing that was now upon Him, and with the personal "hotline" to the Father *(You are my Son, whom I love; with you I am well pleased!)*, Jesus was able to demonstrate the kingdom of God which He did in a powerful way during His ministry over the next approximately 3 ½ years.

The requirements for His ministry on this earth were in no way different to those for the New Covenant sons and daughters born of God[10] through His atonement, and that includes you and me! In the same way heaven opened at

---

[10] In the biblical sense, sons of God are always men *and* women. God as a Spirit is beyond sexuality. For this reason, and for the sake of simplicity, I will refer to sons of God as also meaning and including daughters of God.

the River Jordan over Jesus, heaven has already opened up over us as a result of the atonement of Jesus and the outpouring of the Holy Spirit.

This fact alone greatly challenges us to reach out for a Jesus-like ministry for mankind – a supernatural ministry with signs and wonders and with wisdom and revelation coming to us directly from heaven. We are qualified in at least the same way for this ministry as Jesus was in the Gospels.

During His ministry, Jesus actually had the disadvantage in that no one else besides Him had the Holy Spirit **on** them, and no one else had a hotline to the Father of Glory **within**.

This means that He was unable to build up a "Glory atmosphere" which could have been built up around Him through the presence of born-again sons. There are therefore very few verses in the Gospels that tell of visible manifestations of God's Glory – and in each such case, always limited to only the one person Jesus (e.g. in Luke 9:28 on the so-called "Mount of Transfiguration").

There was no cloud that enshrouded the people around Him, no "faith-strengthening" visible manifestation of supernatural gold dust, heavenly rain or similar, like we nowadays often experience.

Jesus had really completely "shedded" the Glory mantle that He once had had in heaven.

Can you imagine what this must've meant for Jesus Christ? Can you now understand why He once called out in frustration, *You unbelieving and perverse generation, how long shall I stay with you and put up with you?* (Luke 9:41)

And yet, this complete relinquishment, this complete doing without, were the requirements for fulfilling what He Himself foretold in John 14:12, *Very truly I tell you, whoever believes in me will do the works I have been doing, and they will **do even greater things than these, because I am going to the Father.***

To put it precisely, and for the record, *Jesus Christ left the Glory of God behind for a period of time so that – after the atonement was completed and He had returned to heaven – he could thereby entrust us, his followers, with this very Glory, and empower us to do greater works!!*

What love!

This is exactly what Jesus Himself prophetically speaks about in John 17:5, 22, 24:

And now, Father, glorify me in your presence with the glory I had with you before the world began – (that means He had it before He came to the world which was without it!) – Verse 22: *I have given **them*** (which means us) the glory that you gave me, (which He was about to take on again!) *that they may be one as we are one—I in them and you in me... Father, I want those you have given me **to be with me where I am, and to see my glory**, the glory you have given me because you loved me before the creation of the world.*

Jesus is obviously speaking about the heavenly Glory that He was going to return to and that which we, as His followers after the atonement, should be placed into. Thereby, *His* Glory would then become ours.

Can you see it?

The full gospel isn't just about Jesus dying on the cross for the obliteration of our sins, for the healing of our sicknesses and deficiencies, as well as for the deliverance of our bondages[11] – no, it goes much deeper and further than that:

The work of atonement isn't only about being saved, healed and delivered, but also includes the recovery of the habitat of the Glory of God!

In that Jesus gave up His Glory, accepted and took on becoming a servant who continually stood under attack from the devil and the people under his dominion; in that He remained obedient in His walk right to the end on the cross, He thereby tore the curtain forever more which had until that moment separated us from the original habitat of God's Glory. As a result he made it possible for us, as children of God, to permanently live in and out of the Glory of the Father!

---

[11] Although this is naturally all included in the atonement and is most important, many books, however, have already been written about these aspects!

There was a reason for the awesome sign in the temple at the moment of Jesus's death – the curtain that symbolically divided ordinary people from the Glory of God (the Holy of Holies), was torn in two parts (Matthew 27:51)!

"RECOGNIZE MY HUMANITY"

In spring 2013, when I had returned to my hotel room between two Glory and Miracle Services, I had been praying for some time kneeling by my bed when suddenly I perceived Jesus on the other side of the bed. He looked directly at me and all He said was, "Recognize my humanity" and then disappeared.

I was completely taken aback because, at first, I couldn't make out what Jesus was trying to tell me.

However, because it doesn't happen often that I clearly see Jesus standing opposite me, I knew that there must be a profound meaning hidden in this sentence which I hadn't, as yet, been able to comprehend, and so I meditated again and again on this statement over the following months.

In the meantime, I believe that this request from Jesus to recognize His "humanity" holds a wealth of meaning.

One that most certainly pertains to this is that Jesus, the unique son of God, became totally human (the Son of Man) – outside of the Glory environment of the Father – thereby paving the way that we, through Him and His atonement, can become sons of God within the Glory environment.

In the spirit it is already accomplished ("It is finished!"). It is now up to us to understand, to grasp this spiritual reality and allow it to become more and more a part of our lives.

You could also put it this way – with only the anointing of the Holy Spirit on Him and an untarnished personal relationship to the Father, Jesus demonstrated what is possible here on earth for a "Son of man" who is anchored in heaven – so that we can now demonstrate what is possible on the earth through firmly anchored "sons of God" in Christ, in and from the habitat of Glory! With that, we are doing exactly the works that He did and even greater things than these (John 14:12).

In bringing many sons and daughters to glory, it was fitting that God, for whom and through whom everything exists, should make the pioneer of their salvation perfect through what he suffered. Hebrews 2:10

God suffered for us as Son of man in order to lead us, as the sons of God, to Glory! He came in the form of a servant so that we can take on the form of sons.

Jesus became a Son of man outside of the Glory so that we can become sons of God within the Glory!

He left the Glory behind for a period of time to make it possible that we, starting right here and now, are able to have a life in this Glory in all eternity.

If that isn't good news!

In all eternity our Lord Jesus Christ will be given all honor for this awesome work of salvation. And all the more so, when the effects of this powerful act of love become visible on us, the believers.

Now is the time when the Body of Christ becomes conscious that the Glory is its actual habitat, and learns to live in it continually. We live in the very last era of mankind before Jesus comes again!

And in these end times the Holy Spirit won't rest until we, as followers of the glorious Lamb of God, have claimed and manifested everything which He, through an unimaginable price, acquired for us! Legally speaking it belongs to us already.

For this purpose, here's a little illustration:

About a year ago, God showed me in a vision of a little grasshopper. This grasshopper was continually tickled from behind with a little stick but, typical of a grasshopper, it couldn't be bothered to jump! It was tickled and tickled again and again until, being fed up, made the expected jump forward!

God spoke to me and explained that the Body of Christ is like this grasshopper. It'll be "tickled" again and again by the Holy Spirit, and by the fresh revelations we receive out of the Word of God, until it leaves all sluggishness behind and jumps forward, just like God intended. The time for this is, in fact **now!**

God wants to see us doing awesome things! Only in this way can Jesus receive all the honor He deserves for His amazing act of love! It's not enough to just confess, "Jesus, I give you honor" but rather it is time to see His Glory manifested in our lives by doing His supernatural works in this world! That is what will **truly** honor him!

The following experience illustrates this:

When I was in France in 2014, I was having a great time in praise and worship when suddenly a prophetic view into heaven opened up. In my vision I intuitively knew that I was seeing the end of my life as I saw a multitude of angels and the "cloud of witnesses" applauding Jesus for all He had accomplished on this earth through me. I immediately knew that this is exactly the goal I am living for. I am the one taking hold of it and living it out, but Jesus will be the one receiving all the honor.

Now is the time to take on the challenge and, led by the Holy Spirit, to go deeper into the knowledge of God (Philippians 3:8) discovering our possibilities as sons in His Glory.

The habitat of Glory that was destined for you since the beginning of creation is completely open to you – there is no longer any reason not to learn to live in it, and from out of it.

Your journey begins NOW…

SUMMARY

- The sending of Jesus Christ from out of God's Glory and His work of atonement were necessary in order to terminate the separation of mankind from the heavenly Glory once and for all.

- The "full" gospel includes the fact that Jesus not only restored to us our righteousness, our freedom and our health, but also our original environment – the Glory of God.

- Jesus gave up His Glory with the Father so that we, through Him, can step into the Glory – and therefore accomplish even greater things than He was able to do here on earth.

- Jesus became a complete son of man outside of the Glory so that we can become sons of God within the Glory.

10

How the Full Gospel

Affects Us

As we have seen, the separation of mankind from God's Glory, man's original environment for thousands of years, has been removed through the Person Jesus Christ and His work of redemption – the curtain is torn.

In the spirit this is an unalterable fact. If we live according to the spirit instead of our natural senses (Galatians 5:16), then God's Glory will become a permanent living reality.

For the wages of sin is death, but the gift of God is eternal life in Christ Jesus our Lord. (Romans 6:23)

The consequences of Adam's sin was a life under the power of death, i.e. a life *outside* of God's Glory. Through Jesus Christ, however, we have been given new, eternal life, i.e. a life *in* the glory.

The term "eternal life" not only implies that this life lasts for eternity – the Greek word "zoe" for life talks about a completely different godly (glorious) **quality** of new life.

This Life becomes a part of us when we personally receive Jesus into our lives and believe in His atonement: *Yet to all who did receive him, to those who believed in his name, he gave the right to become children of God—* (John 1:12)

THE STATE OF RIGHTEOUSNESS

This new life that we receive is linked to a whole new state in God – the state of righteousness.

Even the righteousness of God which is by faith of Jesus Christ unto all and upon all them that believe: for there is no difference: For all have sinned, and come short of the glory of God; Being justified freely by his grace through the redemption that is in Christ Jesus.
(Romans 3:22-24, KJV)

At the moment we accept Jesus Christ as our Savior and receive His work of grace in faith, we are positioned in a state of righteousness before God – without sin, without guilt and without blemish. So there is no need to be ashamed or condemned, or in some way feel bad, inferior or scared in His Presence/His Glory.

The Gospel opened up a completely new quality of life for us in the Spirit – a life in and out of the Glory of God!

The environment of God's Glory, His Being, and His manifested presence, are open and accessible for us, without us having to tremble with fear like the people of Israel during the time of Moses (read Hebrews 12:18-24).

The curtain has come down and, through believing this wonderful news, we can move forward here and now into the real, supernatural life in the Glory with all its effects.

During the Old Covenant era it was dangerous to enter into the manifest presence of God[12] because of the abysmal wickedness of mankind. But now, in the New Covenant, we can freely enter into the environment of God's Glory without fear (Hebrews 10:19 onwards).

Because of the original sin, in the Old Covenant the Glory had to be hidden from the perception of mankind – note that Moses's face was veiled (2 Corinthians 3:13). However, in the New Covenant we can, being made righteous (2 Corinthians 5:21), behold the glory with unveiled faces (2

---

[12]This was also the reason why only chosen priests were allowed to enter the Holy of Holies after special preparation on particular days – see Leviticus 16

Corinthians 3:18). This means that the requirements for the fulfillment of the prophecy from Habakkuk 2:14 have now been met completely, and there is no reason why *the earth shouldn't be filled with the knowledge of the glory of the Lord as the waters cover the sea!*

Experiencing the Glory of God is simply a part of our new life and a consequence of our state of righteousness that we have received.

FAITH – THE KEY!

Maybe you are now saying, "Okay, I am now a new creation in Christ and am righteous in Him – and yet I can't always perceive God's Glory. Why is that?

Do I possibly still need a sovereign decision from God to manifest His perceptible Glory here on earth for me?

In order to answer this question we once again need to keep in mind the difference between the Old and New Covenant.

Because of the sin of Adam and Eve, all mankind was automatically completely separated from God before the work of redemption by Jesus. They were not "sons" of God but servants to whom God, by His personal decision, would either sovereignly reveal Himself or not.

His willingness thereby depended mainly on keeping His laws and commandments – it was the Covenant of the Law.

The New Covenant is, however, a much "better covenant" (Hebrews 8:6). It is based on the already accomplished preliminary work of the substitutional atonement of Jesus Christ (thus the pure grace of God!), and is implemented only through faith – and not through keeping laws.

The New Covenant is much better than the old – grace rules and the faith of God in us is the key to the treasure vaults of Glory!

For it is by grace you have been saved, through faith—and this is not from yourselves, it is the gift of God (Ephesians 2:8)

This means that in the Old Covenant any initiative for the revelation of God had to come directly and solely from Him, man for his part could only try to qualify through being on his best behavior. In the New Covenant we only need to believe that we have entered into a completely new relationship with God – the relationship of sons with their Father.

The Spirit you received does not make you slaves, so that you live in fear again; rather, the Spirit you received brought about your adoption to sonship. And by him we cry, "Abba, Father."
(Romans 8:15)

As sons and co-heirs with Jesus Christ (Romans 8:17), as new creations in Christ (2 Corinthians 5:17), God includes us completely in His actions on earth by promising us, for example, *Everything is possible for one **who believes*** (Mark 9:23). Therefore Jesus tells us that we who are in the New Covenant can and should "raid heaven" (Matthew 11:12).

The "currency" of the New Covenant with which you can have everything that God has is *faith*. However, faith is a gift that we receive through the new birth and which is made effective by God's love (Galatians 5:6) – not through perfect behavior.

God can sovereignly take action and sovereignly manifest Himself at any time (and He does time and again even today), but **we** are His main New Covenant project – His sons whom He wants to see emerge in His Glory (Romans 8:19; 1 Corinthians 2:7).

That is why God, once and for all, took the initiative by sending Jesus (Hebrews 1:1-3) – that is His *Grace*! The initiative now lies with us, the *believers*, the sons of God in Christ!

One could also say that Jesus sat down at the right hand of God after having accomplished His mission – now it's up to us here on earth as we have received the spirit of sonship through Him.

The answer to the question whether God's Glory can manifest so that we can perceive it anytime, anywhere, is a definite "yes", wherever sons of God in Christ *believe* in the Full Gospel (as I described in the last section). That means they aggressively take a hold of His real and powerful presence, the heavenly air of Eden, through faith, in the Spirit *here and now*.

The barrier to the awareness of the Glory of God on earth has already completely fallen *by faith* – the curtain is irreversibly torn.

Based on this truth, if only one son of God in Christ by faith seizes the manifested Glory of God and consciously opens himself in the Spirit to the awareness of the glory then it will automatically become increasingly real to him. This will happen for his spiritual senses as well as, depending on the situation and plan of God, for his natural senses – and thus as a direct supernatural break-in by God into this world.

As a child of God you are 100 % qualified for a life in His supernatural Glory through the finished work of Jesus.

God works directly with you in order to manifest His Glory in the earth.

As an example, I have experienced quite a number of times the Holy Spirit making it clear to me that, as a leader of a church service, it strongly depends on me as to whether He will work wonders or manifest certain signs of His Glory or not. If I'm satisfied when nothing supernatural is happening and, spiritually speaking, I'm passive about it then on most occasions nothing will happen. However, if I quasi "press into" the realm of miracles through faith (e.g. proclaim and release specific things, and give the Holy Spirit room to perform certain things, and just don't give up) then these things will happen. This doesn't at all mean that I myself am the author of these works –gold dust raining in a church service, or creative healing miracles happening – but I can, in the Spirit, "position" myself, and the congregation, so that God can do these things.

I remember very clearly one instance where the Holy Spirit rebuked me when I wanted to forego releasing certain miracles because of the "closed" atmosphere. He said, 'You are the leader and therefore you have the authority to lead the congregation into the realm of "openness" where miracles happen. If they don't take place then don't blame the congregation – it's your responsibility!'

You can imagine how this rebuke "pushed" me to do my job properly and not to be satisfied with anything less than the full measure of God's manifestation in that church service.

God does not want to put you under pressure with such an exhortation, but rather wants to show you just how much honor and authority you have in His eyes through Christ.

On the other hand, faith is revealed in certain situations when we are prompted to do nothing except **wait** for God's initiative. Only when we distinctly feel that God's Glory has started moving do we in faith begin to move with Him. How we decide in each particular instance results from the individual leading of the Holy Spirit.

Generally, it's most important that you always take hold of God's Glory in faith and, at the same time, let yourself be totally led by the Holy Spirit – beyond your own understanding.

True faith empowers us to take the initiative, as well as, where necessary, to being able to wait for the heavenly initiative.

Once not only a few individuals but an increasing number of sons of God take hold of this reality *together in faith* and just let themselves "fall into" it, then the impact will be even more powerful and beyond imagination.

The appearance of a visible cloud, or supernaturally glowing faces would belong to the less spectacular manifestations – after all Paul says in 2 Corinthians 3:7-11 that the manifestation of the Glory in the Old Covenant is nothing in comparison with what has been promised for the New Covenant.

By this we realize that, as the Body of Christ we are at the beginning of an awesome journey of discovery lying ahead of us, until the glory of our house, the temple of the Holy Spirit, is exceeding the one of old. This means it is then greater than the glory of the Old Covenant and even that of the early church.

Not until this glory is manifested in full measure will Jesus come again:

Heaven must receive him until the time comes for God to restore everything, as he promised long ago through his holy prophets.
(Acts 3:21)

The (small) beginnings are already visible (even for the natural man).On several occasions, people have already given witness that during our church services they saw a cloud in the room, or above the stage. At fairly regular intervals the manifestation of gold dust, gold and silver glitter or multicolored particles are found on the floor, on the wall, or on the clothes of people attending the service – these all being signs of God's Glory!

Recently, silver glitter manifested in the middle of a large decoration in the form of a heart in our church. It is still there to be marveled at.

Some people who come to our church have given witness to having experienced raindrops manifesting on their arms – a sign for the supernatural glory rain. Others found little gem stones on the floor – a sign from God showing us how precious we are to Him. Many have also experienced supernatural oil on their hands or scalp as a sign for the anointing.

Oftentimes we have also experienced a supernatural wind starting to blow in certain areas of the hall, and also the manifestation of little angels' feathers.

The righteousness of God qualifies you for the journey – your faith is the fuel.

I believe that these (next to all the other miracles and healings of which you will read about later on) are only a few first signs of that which is to come, as more of the Glory of God manifests on this earth through the sons of God. It has definitely begun!

The **qualification** for this journey is the righteousness of God, which you already have become in Jesus (2 Corinthians 5:21[13]).

The **"fuel"** or the **"travel fare"** is the faith that has been given to you through Jesus Christ – ultimately His faith within you.

...*Even the righteousness of God which is by faith of Jesus Christ unto all and upon all them that believe* (Romans 3:22 - KJV)

---

[13]God made Him who had no sin to be sin for us, so that in Him we might become the righteousness of God.

And Galatians 3:22: *But the scripture hath concluded all under sin, that the promise by faith of Jesus Christ might be given to them that believe.* (KJV)

That is why Jesus prophetically also said to us, the sons of the New Covenant, *"Did I not tell you that if you believe, you will see the glory of God?"* (John 11:40).

Faith in the Full Gospel is here and now the solution to the problem regarding the habitat mankind has had since the fall. Through faith we now have the awareness of our position in the habitat that was meant for us right from the beginning (Ephesians 2:6). There is nothing blocking an (everlasting) life in God's "glory bubble" beginning already here and now on earth – just believe His word and it starts[14].

THE GLORY IN YOU AND AROUND YOU

With all this, another spiritual fact works in our favor. While Adam and Eve were in Eden they "only" experienced God's Glory as the environment *around* them. In the New Covenant, however, we have a vital advantage in that we have received Jesus Christ and thereby have God as a Person living *within* us with His Glory.

You are the temple of His Holy Spirit (1 Corinthians 6:19). You could also say that *you* are the tabernacle who keeps the Ark of the Covenant, the manifest Glory of God *within.* You are the dwelling place of God Himself and thereby also of His presence. What a privilege!

You could also put it this way – Eden's environment of glory has not only opened up *around you* through faith, but you actually also carry the environment of Eden *in you.* That is why Paul says, *Christ **in** you, the hope of glory – that is the mystery of God* (Colossians 1:27). His Glory fills you **and** is at the same time around you – wow!

It comes *out of you* and it continually *permeates* all the pores of your being!

---

[14]Please take note that this does not go against the fact that the final, complete and uninterrupted manifestation of God's Glory in the whole world is still to come. This belongs to the new heaven and new earth that will come at the end of time through Jesus (Revelation 21 and 22)! However, we are moving more and more towards the final fulfillment and we therefore shouldn't be surprised that it increasingly becomes a reality.

Christ (the personified Glory) – *is all, and is in all* (Colossians 3:11).

Figuratively speaking, you could explain the difference between Adam in the Garden of Eden and you in Christ by saying that Adam was a closed vessel that was dipped in water – the water being a picture of the glory. The water surrounds the vessel on all sides but doesn't fill it.

As a child of the New Covenant you are not only surrounded by God's Glory but also completely filled with it!

You, as a son of the New Covenant, and part of the last Adam (Christ), are like an open vessel that is immersed in water (the substance of glory) and you are surrounded and filled at the same time.

Looking at it like that we can, from today's point of view, be "glad" that Adam sinned – because without the fall of mankind and the resulting eternal plan of God's work of atonement, we would never have attained this level of existence and these privileges of sonship!

We can only marvel at God's unfathomable depth of wisdom (Romans 11:33). From the beginning He had an eternal and perfect plan – including the anticipated "accident" of the fall of mankind.

GLORY!

SUMMARY

- Through Jesus's accomplished atonement we received the status of perfect righteousness before God. With this, we have permanent and complete freedom to fearlessly enter into the Glory of the Father.

- By faith alone we can live permanently in and through God's Glory and thus experience that His Glory manifests through us on this earth to its full potential.

- We, at the same time, benefit from the fact that we don't just have the Glory around us as a habitat – like Adam – but that, through Christ, have it living "in us". This means that we are the dwelling place of the manifest Glory of God.

11

A NEW CREATION

Therefore, if anyone is in Christ, the new creation has come: The old has gone, the new is here!
(2 Corinthians 5:17)

The real meaning of the reality described in this verse for our new lives in God's Glory cannot be overestimated.

As mentioned already, Jesus, the matchless Son of God, in His endless, all surpassing love which is far above human understanding, gave up His godliness for a period of time and took on the form of our humanity. His goal was to lift us humans up so that we, created beings, could take on the nature of God which means that we actually become a completely new "man" (another translation for a new "creation"). We are not just ordinary people anymore, and we are also not God[15],but rather something totally new – too difficult to grasp for our minds. On one hand we are people with both feet on the ground here on earth and, on the other hand, spiritually speaking, we are already at home in heaven. Terms like "children of God" (Romans 8:14), "participators of the divine nature" (2 Peter 1:4), beings that are "like" Jesus (1 John 4:17), "Temples of God's spirit" (1 Corinthians 3:16) or "houses of Glory" (Haggai 2:9) are some descriptions for us as brand new creations in Christ.

---

[15]Which would be a classic false doctrine!

In John 10:34 Jesus quoted in connection with these new "species", of whom He is the first born, from Psalm 82:6 where it says, *"I said, 'You are "gods"; you are all sons of the Most High.'* Of course this is outrageous and it's no wonder that the religious Jews wanted to stone Jesus for saying such things!

Nevertheless, please take note that we, as sons of God, **cannot** use this verse to refer to us as "God" – only the Father, Jesus Himself and the Holy Spirit are God. **However,** God made the way free for us through the atonement of Jesus to move up to the "league of being" **like** God – because **as** He is, so are we in this world (1 John 4:17 KJV).

When Jesus, being God, talks about us as sons of God saying, "You are gods" then He's here talking about the dimension of the new life that He has made accessible in Himself for us as transformed new creations. Jesus talks about us as His representatives here on earth through whom He wants to raise up His Kingdom – so to speak little "gods" through whom the One mighty God operates – and whereby we become true humans for the first time. I am aware that also this statement almost sounds heretical for religious ears, but I can't change that it is fully biblical.

We have to take hold of these new creation realities in faith, otherwise we will never be able to step out of a religious consciousness, e.g. of being a "sinner who has been forgiven". 2 Corinthians 5:21 says very clearly that someone who takes the atonement of Jesus really seriously, in other words grasps it in faith, **is** no longer a sinner! It is clear-cut in the New Testament that the new creations in Christ have come forth completely from being sinners to being righteous (see Romans 3:22-26; Romans 5:1-2; Romans 8:1-2; 2 Corinthians 5:21; Ephesians 2:1-10; Colossians 1:12-14 and many more). There is no "Not being one, nor being the other", between "the righteous" and "the sinner"!

This reality of the new creation initially only pertains to our **spirit,** and is thereby completely independent from the renewal process that the body and soul of a new creation in Christ naturally still needs here on earth.

It is completely correct that life without Jesus dwelling within our hearts can be described as the life of a sinner and thus as "worm-like". However, if we, being in Christ, still continue to see ourselves as sinners and worms, describing ourselves as such and, even in some cases sing about it, then this actually means we are robbing Jesus of the fruit of His suffering! By doing this we actually curse the new creation that God has made in His love and through His perfect plan of redemption, and hinder it from stepping out and developing its influence in this world.

God created a new "species" in Christ who, in His likeness, represent Him on this earth.

God has chosen to demonstrate His Glory on this earth in a mighty and awesome way before He will let Jesus end this era. He won't do this without His sons, His new creation. This is why we must become entirely conscious of our standing and new being as representatives of Christ on earth.

The revelation of God's sons precedes the ultimate creation of a new heaven and a new earth (Revelation 21). In the Spirit they are already a part of this new world (Romans 8:19).

Therefore, if anyone is in Christ, the new creation has come (2 Corinthians 5:17)

In the millennial reign (Revelation 20), followed by the completely new creation of heaven and earth, God only finishes that which we, as revealed sons of God, have already started on His behalf, here and now.

For this purpose, we need to know who we are; we must learn to live in and out of this (new) state of being. Setting free the glory in the New Covenant no longer primarily happens from the outside through a sovereign act of God like in the Old Covenant. Rather, it occurs from "the inside out", out of the spirit of God's sons, the representatives of the new creation in Christ.

John 7:38 Whoever believes in me, as Scripture has said, rivers of living water will flow from within them (literally from the "belly").

And John 4:14 But whoever drinks the water I give them will never thirst. Indeed, the water I give them will become in them a spring of water welling up to eternal life.

You have to realize who you are through and in Christ, and then you only need to set free this reality in faith out of your innermost being. The result is that life in abundance will come forth and spread out all around you.

The life of God always flows "from the inside out".

Ezekiel 36:26-27 is a prophecy concerning the new creation:

I will give you a new heart and put a new spirit in you; I will remove from you your heart of stone and give you a heart of flesh. And I will put my Spirit in you and move you to follow my decrees and be careful to keep my laws.

Here, Ezekiel prophecies what will happen at the moment when an individual personally gives Jesus Christ reign over his life. He receives in his innermost being the heart of God, the Spirit of God, who is altogether God Himself. John 1:12 *Yet to all who did receive him, to those who believed in his name, he gave the right to become children of God.*

This revolution, even more so this complete renewal and metamorphosis, takes place at first not on the outside, but rather on the inside of a person.

1 Peter 3:4 (KJV) calls this *the hidden man of the heart.*

This hidden man of the heart, which is man's spirit, is, because of the fall of mankind, partaker of the nature of Satan. But, at the very moment when Jesus Christ enters him, he becomes partaker of the nature of God (2 Peter 1:4). That is the Gospel!

If you already made Jesus the Lord of your life, then you can now confess "I am a partaker of the nature of God. I am newly created in Christ by God, and I now have His heart. I no longer live, but Christ lives in me!"

Please note, initially the outward man remains exempt from this recreation – the new creation doesn't take place in the body (which is obvious), neither does it take place in our soul, i.e. our intellect, our feelings and our human will – although it will have immediate effects on these.

Our soul and our body have to first be renewed *"in knowledge after the image of him that created him"* (Colossians 3:9-10 KJV; and see also Romans 12:1-2 etc.). This happens automatically out of our already newly created spirit if we align to and concentrate on our inner (spiritually new) person, instead of on the outer man.

You can release this reality within you by embracing the following confession: "I concentrate on Jesus in me and release His life from my spirit – rivers of living water are now flowing from out of my inner being – for my soul, my body and all of my environment."

God created man as a three-part being, whereby his spirit is his actual essence because it is here where the image of God is found (contrary to animals which have no spirit because they are not created in the image of God).

This spiritual being of man **has** a soul and **lives** in a body.

We are a spirit, have a soul and live in a body.

In the new birth, our spirit is newly created, receives a new nature (namely the nature of God) while the old nature dies in the spirit on the cross with Christ and is thereby finished with ("past"). Out of our newly created spirit, our soul and our body (our "dwelling place") are then continually transformed into the same image.

This complete recreation is thus the most revolutionary occurrence since the foundation of the world, and the ultimate crowning of God's plan for mankind. It greatly exceeds the significance and impact of the creation of mankind in the Garden of Eden – in heaven as well as on earth.

No wonder that even God's angels have, for thousands of years, waited impatiently for the revelation of this secret (1 Peter 1:12).

We cannot allow ourselves to minify this mighty spiritual reality of our new being. Instead, we should eagerly study it, meditate on it, confess it and make ourselves conscious of it – along with the resulting consequences. Doing this, we eventually become our new self in Christ, i.e. He Himself manifesting more and more in all that we are and do on earth.

We must understand that the greatest joy that lay ahead of Jesus which made His suffering on the cross endurable (Hebrews 12:2) was not about heaven (He knew heaven already, and in order to get there He had no need to suffer on the cross) but rather that **we**, you and I, the new creation, the sons of

God, would come forth as fruit from the kernel of wheat that fell to the ground and died (John 12:24).

> **The greatest joy that lay ahead of Jesus, which made His suffering on the cross endurable, was the new creation – that is you and I who represent Him here on this earth.**

The Father in heaven wanted a family (not just **an only** son), and He sent His matchless son as a kernel of wheat into the world to acquire this family.

The revelation of God's sons as new creations was thus the dream of Jesus, enabling Him to endure the spiritually dead people around Him, and then the death on the cross, including the time of separation from the Father.

It is our privilege to be available for Him for His dream to become reality. Believe it – confess it – release it – and experience it!

THE "SUBSTANCE" OF THE NEW CREATION

The new creation that replaced our old, natural self, enslaved by the nature of Satan, consequently contains everything that Jesus IS – everything that is in Him, everything that He has, everything that He is, everything that He does and can do.

Galatians 2:20a I have been crucified with Christ and I no longer live, but Christ lives in me. 1 John 4:17b, In this world we are like Jesus. Colossians 3:10b: being renewed in knowledge in the image of its Creator.

> **Everything that Jesus is, is now already in you.**

Since Jesus Christ is God then this new life that we now have also is by nature completely unending, inexhaustible, and it probably never can be conveyed sufficiently with human words:

The Jesus kind of love dwells in us (Romans 5:5), just like His joy (Hebrews 1:9), His righteousness (2 Corinthians 5:21), His peace (Ephesians 2:14), His wisdom and His Holiness (1 Corinthians 1:30), His Glory (John 17:22), His wealth (2 Corinthians 8:9), and, and, and – the list continues on endlessly!

The complete fullness of God dwells and is alive through Christ in *you*. Can you now see why Jesus quoted in John 10:34: *you are Gods…!?*

It is now up to us to learn to let this abundance emerge from our innermost being to take over our souls, and our bodies. We do this by faith in the truth of His word. Thus we bless mankind and the world around us with all of this glory, and take them along into this mightiest of all transformation processes which has already begun from heaven above.

FROM WITHIN AND FROM ABOVE

The ministry of the new creation always happens from within – and, also, at the same time, from above, i.e. from heaven.

The new creation actually contains God Himself, and with it all of heaven.

In your spirit (as you are already a completely newly created being) you can at any time be here on earth as well as in heaven at the same time.

Jesus Himself revealed this reality when He said in John 3:13 (KJV): And no man hath ascended up to heaven, but he that came down from heaven, even the Son of man which is in heaven.

In other words, Jesus said: I, as the son of God, have come out of heaven and stand now here before you on earth, but, at the same time, I am in heaven. Jesus was the "first born among many brothers" – one could also say the role model for the new creation that we are now through Him. This then means that it is a characteristic of our nature as new creations to live in heaven and on earth at the same time – quasi "bi-dimensional".

You are living on earth and in heaven at the same time.

This is confirmed in Ephesian 2:4-7 *But because of his great love for us, God, who is rich in mercy, made us alive with Christ even when we were dead in transgressions—it is by grace you have been saved. And God raised us up with Christ and **seated us with him in the heavenly realms** in Christ Jesus, in order that in the coming ages he might show the incomparable riches of his grace, expressed in his kindness to us in Christ Jesus.*

We have to spiritually grasp that, as new creations, we haven't only been made one in the spirit with the death of Jesus (regarding the old man), and His resurrection from the dead, but also with His ascension into heaven to be seated at the right hand of the Father, and thus with the heavenly life that He now leads there. Our identification with Christ pertains to His whole atonement – from the cross to the throne!

We were therefore buried with him through baptism into death in order that, just as Christ was raised from the dead through the glory of the Father, **we too may live a new life.** (Romans 6:4)

This new life that Paul talks about here is the exact same life as in Ephesians 2:6 (see above). It takes place in the heavenly realms and should, in the time remaining until the return of Jesus, be visible through us, and thereby become the answer to Jesus's prayer: *Your kingdom come, your will be done, on earth as it is in heaven (Matthew 6:10).*

The new creation (you!) has free access permanently to God's Holy Place (Hebrews 10:19), which means to the heavenly throne room, to the heavenly realms and also to all the blessings that are in heaven (Ephesians 1:3 *Praise be to the God and Father of our Lord Jesus Christ, who has blessed us in the heavenly realms with every spiritual blessing in Christ).*

You have a direct line to the very top and you thereby are a full shareholder of the life of Christ which He leads at the right hand of the Father in heaven. For some ears this might sound a bit strange but that is the exact meaning when the Holy Spirit in us is referred to as the "deposit of our inheritance" (which is heaven) (Ephesians 1:14).

More than a 100 years ago, John G. Lake advanced into the depths of this revelation and, as a result, can surely be counted as a father and forerunner to God's on-going glory movement. In 1910 he was used by the Holy Spirit during a sermon on this topic to deliver a message in tongues, which was subsequently interpreted in front of the congregation as follows: *"Christ is at once the spotless descent of God into man and the sinless ascent of man into God. And the Holy Spirit is the agent by which it is accomplished."* A powerful statement which we can also interpret like this: Christ came as the spotless Lamb of God into the world in order to make sinful man righteous and to dwell in him. With this He made it possible for man to ascend, as shareholder of His ascension, into heavenly realms, into God Himself. Wow!

So, once again, declare: "With Christ I am right now translated to heavenly places. I live simultaneously in heaven and on earth. In my spirit I have free access to all heavenly blessings and, in faith, draw them onto the earth. I am completely and utterly like Jesus in this world!"

SUMMARY

- At that moment we receive Jesus we become a new creation, a new "species". The essence of God now lives in a human body with a human soul – representing Jesus Christ – "as He is" on this earth.

- Filled with Christ, we already belong to the new heaven and the new earth that will one day finally replace the earth in its present form. It is our calling to help the new world break-in and break-through into this world here and now.

- This task is fulfilled through our direct link to heaven, "seated in heavenly places in Christ". This connection exists in our newly created spirit – "in our innermost being".

- From there we release heavenly rivers of living water in faith over the people around us in this world.

12

Identifying with the Glorified Christ and Reigning in the Spirit

Isn't it interesting that 1 John 4:17 says that we are like Jesus *is*, and not that we are like Jesus *was*?

Strictly speaking for today, what is Jesus like? Is He a carpenter, thirty years old with brown hair and a long white robe who performs signs and wonders and speaks mighty words? Or actually more like the exalted Christ in power and glory, like He is perceived by John in Revelations 1:12-16?

John 14:12 goes on to say that whoever believes in Him will do the works that He is *doing* (not what he has *done!*). Is this really speaking about the works Jesus *did* in the Gospels– or, rather, what is Jesus *doing* at this moment, there where He is now (in heaven)?

On my journey into Glory it became increasingly clear to me that, on the one hand, it is right and important, as a Christian, to identify with Jesus during His earthly ministry. However, there is also another dimension of spiritual reality in our lives and ministries as new creations and sons of God on the earth. Namely, a life and ministry which flows from the *elevated, heavenly and glorified Christ* how He is *now*, at this moment – *as in heaven so on earth!*

We shouldn't only identify with the works of Jesus on this earth, but rather also with the glorified Jesus at the right hand of the Father.

Please don't misunderstand me at this point. It is an absolutely important and glorious thing to study the Gospels, to deeply empathize with Jesus, and to see yourself doing the same miraculous works we read about Him doing. I preach this and practice it frequently myself.

And if every Christian would just express even a fraction of what Jesus introduced us to in the Gospels in their walk then we have, as the Body of Christ, definitely taken a big step forward.

This means that the revelation of ministering out of the heavenly Christ doesn't in any way replace the revelation of ministering out of the Christ in the Gospels (which is the same Jesus Christ anyway).

This revelation rather complements and completes the first revelation, which we have long been familiar with.

EXCURSUS ON "REVELATION AND THE WRITTEN WORD OF THE BIBLE"

The finished work of atonement in Jesus Christ which has been accomplished two thousand years ago and been revealed to us in the New Testament as the Gospel (=good news) has such an infinite depth that it will keep us busy into all eternity as we try to "unpack" and grasp its truth and revelation in all of its fullness.

You can neither add to, nor subtract, anything from this revelation or the scriptures as the inspired Word of God. The Bible is conclusive and complete. God won't allow another single new book to be written that could come anywhere close to the Bible and its significance and depth (if anyone claims otherwise then he's probably on his way to starting a cult!).

However, at the same time, the Spirit-guided student of the Word is, according to the words of Jesus, one who continually brings out the "new as well as the old" from out of his treasure (Matthew 13:52). In this, the new never replaces the old, but rather completes it.

The revelation of His word is forever *progressing,* because God, and also His Word, are eternal and so they both have an immeasurable depth!

The *new* is that what God reveals *now*, i.e. it is a direct rendition of what is given to us by the Holy Spirit now.

That is why the strongest demonstration of power by the Holy Spirit is always in connection with the new – not with the old (meaning a revelation that was meant for the Body of Christ at an earlier time).

Those who want to experience God today and now in *power and reality* will have to yield to what He *currently* reveals to His church (see Revelations 2:29 *Whoever has ears, let them hear what the Spirit says* (not said!) *to the churches.*

In other words, it is necessary to keep up with what God is currently *doing* and *saying.*

God's revelation to His church is continually in progress and thereby always fresh. Of course every current revelation must have its foundation in the legitimate eternal Word of God.

This however doesn't mean that previous revelations (and especially not the once and for all documented revelation in the bible) suddenly become irrelevant. This error quickly leads to an unhealthy imbalance, fanaticism and spiritual instability.

In fact the Bible says in Psalm 119:160 *The sum of thy word is truth* (DARBY), and in 2 Tim. 3:16 *All Scripture is God-breathed and is useful for teaching...*

Note also that Jesus says that His word is full of the Spirit and life (John 6:63).

To view God's word *detached* from the Spirit of God and from His current movement in the Body of Christ always leads to fruitlessness, zero impact, legalism and splitting of hairs.

Alternatively, separating the Spirit of God from the word of God leads to insubstantial fanaticism which is quick to believe all sorts of things without aligning it to the foundation of the Word! And, before you know it, the spirit in which you move is no longer the Holy Spirit.

Both errors are dangerous and, coming from opposite directions, attempt to rob the Body of Christ of its liveliness and explosive spiritual power.

In order to remain in a healthy framework, I believe, the following "guidelines" that originate from Martin Luther's reformation can help us with regard to all the fresh and new revelations which we gain through the Holy Spirit from Scripture (I am using the original Latin keywords here as characterized by Luther):

1.) Sola scriptura ("by Scripture alone") – which means that there is no other binding written source of revelation than the Bible alone.

2.) Sola gratia ("by grace alone") and sola fide ("through faith alone") – which means the finished work of Jesus Christ for us is the advance payment which every human being has been given undeservedly – it cannot be earned by any work on our part and is grasped by faith alone. This message is called "the Gospel" and it is the central message of the whole Bible *from which everything receives its proper place and into which all things in scripture converge.*

3.) Solus Christus ("Christ alone") – the grace of God, which is the Gospel for us, is revealed only in and through the Person of Jesus Christ. Beyond Him there is no grace and also nothing divine that we could grasp in faith. We could also say: He is at the center of the new creation and the Glory of God. He is the personified Glory of the Lord!

I believe that the last generation before Jesus comes again will be those who stand on the firm and clear foundation of the Holy Scripture, who will interpret it from the center, which means from its correct perspective. They will be the ones accumulating the biggest treasure of divine revelation compared to any previous generation. And that generation will, at the same time, have its ear so close to the heart-beat of the Holy Spirit that they will know what the current revelation of God is for the now and for this era. He will accompany them with the demonstration of His Spirit and His power,

> with signs, wonders and miracles, and with profound reformation and transformation.

So as important and appropriate the imitation of the earthly ministry of Jesus is, so is identifying *with Him the raised and glorified Christ who sits at the right hand of God* equally important for us as new creations – revealed sons of God. This means that we perceive in the Spirit what the glorified One is doing right now, and then do the exact works that we see Him doing – just like Jesus never did anything except that what He saw the Father in heaven doing[16].

John 5:19: Jesus gave them this answer: *"Very truly I tell you, the Son can do nothing by himself; he can do only what he sees his Father doing, because whatever the Father does the Son also does."* Exactly, this is also applicable to us.

And, at the same time, God *wants* to show us all that He is doing at this moment in heaven – otherwise Jesus wouldn't have said immediately in the next verse, John 5:20: *For **the Father loves the Son and shows him all he does**. Yes, and he will show him even greater works than these, so that you will be amazed.*

There is no reason for us as sons of God not to take advantage of this reality for us – and, in the spirit, which is our inner man, to live in heavenly realms (in faith) and perceive there what the Father and the glorified Christ are doing right now. We then do this here on earth as His extended arm.

Let me give you a specific example. A few years ago, we organized an open-air service on the market square in a city called Reutlingen where we were disturbed by a large group of youths on the other side of the market square. They were causing a spectacle by drinking alcohol, shouting and using loud whistles against my preaching. An obviously demon-possessed lady then came up to me and tried to knock the microphone out of my hand while I was

---

[16]It goes without saying that the works of the glorified Christ would never contradict the works of the earthly Jesus like they are revealed in the Gospels. No one will be able to take advantage of the exalted Christ for statements and works that contradict the Word of God, the Bible, in any way.

preaching. In this situation I had no other option than to look to Jesus to see what He would do. He indicated that I should move towards the troublemakers with the whole church group, sit down with them and begin to talk to them about God. Letting my group know this, I put into practice what I saw, went ahead of our group and we all sat down in the middle of the "den of lions". At that moment the whole atmosphere changed. The youths were so perplexed by our boldness and were convicted by God's love. Many of them gave their lives to Jesus, allowed us to pray for them and we had good discussions with them right into the night. God had turned the whole situation around and changed it into a mighty victory!

That is exactly what will happen in the most diverse situations whenever we just look to see what Jesus is doing in the heavenly realms.

The key for exercising our God entrusted dominion over this world in the correct way lies with this new consciousness of sitting with Christ in heavenly realms.

*For if, by the trespass of the one man, death reigned through that one man, how much more will those who receive God's abundant provision of grace and of the gift of righteousness **reign in life through the one man, Jesus Christ!*** (Romans 5:17).

In heaven only One reigns, namely God. If we live in Christ out of the heavenly realms in this world then the lordship of the One will automatically be established more and more on earth through us.

In unity with the glorified Christ we reign from heaven over situations and circumstances that we encounter on this earth.

An illustration: I remember when there was a dispute over a railway project called "Stuttgart 21" which kept the whole region around Stuttgart on their toes for months. Big demonstrations took place in this context which sometimes led to violence. People were injured and when you walked downtown Stuttgart during that time you could feel that the atmosphere was charged with hate.

It was obvious that the devil tried to effectively poison the atmosphere of our city. I had heard the disconcerting news but didn't give it much attention at first. One Tuesday evening during praise and worship in our church God spoke clearly to me, "How long are you actually going to allow the devil to poison the atmosphere in this region? You have been placed here and it is your responsibility to stop this spirit!" I immediately told the congregation what I had heard, and what Jesus obviously wanted to do through us. Together we took authority over the spirits of hate, division, rebellion and violence that the devil had planted into our city. I felt peace in my heart and knew that in the Spirit the matter had now turned.

And so it was – only a few days later a so-called mediator was appointed to deal with this matter. A couple of weeks later I opened the newspaper and saw a photo of this mediator pictured with angel's wings. Over it were the headlines in bold "His sword was the word!" Underneath you could read that the mediator had been successful in calming the situation (I believe it was God working through this man). And since then there have practically been no more traces of the then apparent spirits in our city.

This is only one example of many as to how we govern in Christ from heavenly realms, bringing heaven down to earth and, as a result, influence the history of our city or region. I have often also experienced on a national and even international level how the Holy Spirit worked through me and other sons of God in a similar way.

Jesus's prayer: "Thy kingdom come, thy will be done, on earth as it is in heaven", is therefore being continuously fulfilled.

THE AGE OF TRANSFIGURATION

When we, as a new creation in the spirit, identify ourselves with Christ at the right hand of the Father, then Bible texts like Revelations 1:12-16[17], where

---

[17] *I turned around to see the voice that was speaking to me. And when I turned I saw seven golden lampstands, and among the lampstands was someone like a son of man, dressed in a robe reaching down to his feet and with a golden sash around his chest. The hair on his head was white like wool, as white as snow, and his eyes were like blazing fire. His feet were like bronze glowing in a furnace, and his voice was like the sound of rushing waters. In his right hand he held seven stars, and coming out of his mouth was a sharp, double-edged sword. His face was like the sun shining in all its brilliance.*

Christ is revealed in His full power and Glory, will take on a whole new meaning – that is to say as a revelation *of the indwelling new life,* the new spiritual personality of power and might and Glory of God *that already is within us.*

If we go through this life with an inner consciousness that the glorified Christ lives in us, then things like healing the sick just by our shadows happen much easier, more frequently and more "naturally" than we have experienced in the past.

Yes, ultimately we will no longer be surprised because this will be an automatic result, the automatic overflow of our new being in Christ.

Even in His transfiguration Jesus was a prototype for us. Just like the disciples with Jesus, more and more people will see the radiation of God's Glory shine out of God's sons.

I remember one instance when I was on a ladder in front of our apartment trimming a tree, I did not notice the lady from our church approaching from behind until she called out, "I'm healed, I'm healed!" I then turned around and saw the lady joyfully hopping around on the street. God had healed her only because she came within the sphere of radiation of God's Glory that goes forth from a new creation in Christ! At the time I was completely focused on trimming that tree so that I hadn't noticed what was going on. Every one of us can experience such things more often because in the end it is just a matter of faith and thus of the consciousness that is being brought about by the Word of God *in us.*

In this context it is worth once again studying the transfiguration story in Mark 9:1-8.

We see here how the "Son of Man" Jesus is transfigured in front of His three closest disciples. It says in a parallel passage in Luke 9:29 *As he was praying, the appearance of his face changed, and his clothes became as bright as a flash of lightning.* An undeniably prophetic sign took place here in regard to the coming glorification of Jesus, and there is a direct spiritual connection to Revelations 1:12-16.

However, first of all, I would like to draw your attention to what Jesus says in the verse just before the transfiguration story (Mark 9:1): *And he said to them, Truly I tell you, some who are standing here will not taste death before they see that the kingdom of God has come with power.*

What is Jesus talking about here? This verse, just before the transfiguration of Jesus (you could say as the introduction to it), only makes sense when we understand that the following transfiguration (or "glorification") is a foreshadow of the revelation of the new creation after the Holy Spirit came at Pentecost.

Jesus, as our role model (the firstborn among many brothers – Romans 8:29), gave us a prophetic sign here of the manifestation of the glorified sons of God during the era of the Holy Spirit.

Just as the Glory of God oozed from every pore of Jesus and was "recognized" by his surroundings, so are we also destined to experience how the Glory of God emerges with increasing power out of us so that the people around us – especially the non-believers – will experience it in a mighty way and recognize and perceive Christ in us even with their senses.

And that does indeed make sense. Why else would Paul write in 2 Corinthians 3.7-11 that the glory of the New Covenant is even more glorious than that of the Old, when Moses already had to cover his face so that the radiation of Glory on his countenance did not blind or unsettle the Israelites.

The glory of the new creation, and the sons to be soon revealed should therefore be more powerful, and become more visible than with Moses, right?

I dare to say that Jesus might not come again before this manifestation of His Glory in and through His family has taken place on a large scale here on earth, until more people see the Glory of God, Jesus, God Himself, when they look at us.

In connection with this, I remember something that the Holy Spirit once said to me. He said, "The era of enlightenment is over with, now is the era of transfiguration". During this time the focus is not on mental knowledge and understanding, but on taking hold of the supernatural reality of the glorification of the revealed sons of God!

Please note: This does not mean that we would be in any way special because of ourselves (this cannot be stressed enough). But rather, quite simply, that Jesus, with His complete resurrection Glory, begins to reveal Himself more and more in us based on the total death of our old, egotistic self which was already crucified with Christ 2000 years ago!

It is therefore very important to balance the statements in this chapter with what the Bible says about the renewing of the mind. No one should make the mistake and believe that a completely un-renewed Christian living in the flesh could ever reach this dimension of glory, i.e. reflecting credibly the complete covering and oneness with Christ (see Galatians 5:19-21)!

It doesn't make sense having heard this message once or, just after having read this book, to then tell everyone you meet, "Look at me and you will see the Glory of God!"

The point rather is that, as Christians, we should become more and more conscious of the reality of God's Glory in us – *and also* of the reality of our complete death to the inclinations of the un-renewed soul and flesh. We are accordingly thus renewing our thoughts, and progressively come in line with the Word of God.

We will then experience with all the more intensity how this new glory-consciousness progressively takes over and saturates our external man. And, without having to draw attention to ourselves, people around us will perceive and experience this heavenly reality about us (also in the form of healing, encouragement, miracles) and consequently be drawn to Jesus whom they see working in us.

Didn't Jesus say? John 12:32 – *And I, when I am lifted up from the earth, will draw all people to myself.*

Jesus made this statement before the coming of the Holy Spirit.

As we are now in the era of the Holy Spirit, you can, after what we have now said about the new creation, put it like this: *And I* (Jesus), *when I am lifted up within the innermost being of the sons of God, in their hearts, I will draw,* **through them,** *all people to myself.*

Or take the following verse which summarizes this all very well:

Colossians 3:3-4: *For you died* (to the natural), *and your life* (the new) *is now hidden with Christ in God* (in the spiritual heavenly realm). *When Christ, who is your life, appears, then you also will appear with him in glory.*

This manifestation is already happening now in our time through the Holy Spirit in that we become conscious of this reality by believing the Word of God!

Transfiguration experiences like the disciples had with Jesus will therefore become more frequent for the people around the sons of God...

The prophecy by the late Kenneth E. Hagin which he gave a few years before his death in around the turn of the millennium, fits very well here (translated from the German version):

<<In the last days there will be those who will walk this earth like God. They will speak like God and act like God. Religious people will accuse and ridicule them, saying, "They think that they are something special, they even think that they are God." And the Spirit of God says, "No, they are not God. They are children of God, messengers of God that have been sent out to perform the works of God."

In this hour, at this time, you and I will take our places and the world will be amazed. They could never have imagined that, in their eyes, an ordinary person could walk with such power and authority.>>

In the end times, sons and daughters of God will stand up and walk the earth "like God".

<<Yeah, a new breed will rise up and go forward. They will not fear the devil. They have no fear of people and they will speak in boldness and challenge the strongholds of the devil. And there will be great trembling but those standing firmly on the Rock will rejoice over the storm.

And this Body will get up just like a huge giant; he'll shake off everything that hinders him and break the bondage of traditions and religion that have held him back.

A new group of people will arise in these days, a brand new breed. An army of men and women will rise. They know their rights and privileges in Christ and they will walk in all that already belongs to them.>>

Bear in mind that in all this our natural man is completely irrelevant – it isn't more (or less) – than the glove for God and His Glory, a submissive vessel which the Master can use for His fullness and power.

It's not about the building up of our ego, it's not about awareness of *self* but it's about the death of our ego and *God-consciousness!*

The more Christians receive this awareness, the more powerful the movement of His Holy Spirit which we are now entering into will become – the manifestation of the Glory of God in and through the sons of God with signs and wonders and mighty deeds. And this will accelerate the coming in of the last great harvest like nothing else!

Amen!

SUMMARY

- As a new creation in Christ we are not only called to identify with the earthly Jesus we know in the Gospels. Rather we also identify with the already glorified Christ at the right hand of God (see Revelations 1:12-16). We look to Him in us and put into action on earth that what we see Him doing.

- As a result of identifying with the glorified Christ we will grow in the consciousness of the Glory of God being in us and around us. We will then experience more and more how His Glory radiates through us and from us – which means that we consequently are "revealed" as the glorified sons of God in the Spirit – for this world. This also means that through us the dominion of God over this planet will become newly erected and visible.

- Even if our appearance for some seems to be "God-like" we are still absolutely and completely aware of the fact that we are not God, but rather God's vessels – not more and not less.

13

FROM THE GLORY TO THE

HARVEST

I lay on my back on the floor of my office and was focused completely on God. Praise and worship music was playing in the background and the presence of God in the room was strong. Suddenly the Holy Spirit opened the eyes of my heart and a film began to play which I was a part of.

At the beginning, a mighty pyramid-shaped mountain came rolling towards me – it reminded me of a huge throne on which the king "rideth". I knew intuitively that it was the Glory of the Father's throne.

This glory virtually rolled over me, flattening me out on the floor and I knew immediately that this was the end of my old, carnal man.

After this "mountain" had completely rolled over me a smaller mountain appeared behind. On the top I recognized the victorious Lamb with the banner of the cross, and I promptly knew that behind this mountain lay the land of my personal calling.

The unification with the victorious Lamb of God is the requirement for reaching the land of our calling.

At first I tried to get around the mountain but that wasn't possible. I then searched for a tunnel through the mountain but there wasn't one. Finally, I knew that I had no other choice other than to climb up to the peak. When I arrived at the top, the Lamb of God was standing there and I felt that I must embrace Him. Suddenly I was rolling down the other side of the mountain closely entwined with the Lamb.

I had to completely unite with the slaughtered and victoriously resurrected Lamb in order to reach the land of my destiny.

When I stood up on the other side of the mountain I looked in front of me and saw a beautiful country – on one side it was a luscious green and on the other side a deep golden yellow of a ripe harvest – it was wonderful!

At that moment in the vision I thought of a dream I had had as a 5 year old boy (probably the only spiritual dream of my whole childhood). In this dream I was driving a combine harvester through golden yellow harvest fields when suddenly, between the ripe ears, the devil showed his grotesque face. However, in the dream I just drove over the devil and "chopped him up" under the blades of my combine harvester!

While I was still in my vision looking at the ripe and fruitful land before me, I was thinking about this dream and I saw in front of me three words that were connected with hyphens – *Glory-Harvest-International.*

Immediately I knew in my spirit, "Yes, that's it!" The harvest will be brought in from out of the glory and it will be international – worldwide!

Then the film ended and since that time I have pondered a lot about its spiritual message. In the process, God has shown me the following aspects:

1. When the Glory of God abides in our lives then the natural man cannot remain standing upright (see 1 Kings 8:10-11 KJV, when the glory cloud filled Solomon's temple so that the priests could not stand to minister). The natural man would, in fact, be completely "flattened" until all movement of our carnal nature is eliminated.

2. The Glory of God the Father is always also the Glory of the Lamb, i.e. of Jesus. Without being unified with Him we cannot see the calling the Holy Spirit has for our lives, let alone walk in it.

3. This calling comes into being in full measure only out of the Glory of God – never detached from it or without it.

However, when the Body of Christ learns to live out of the glory then it will bring in the harvest of souls that God has predetermined for the end times before the return of Jesus – and it will be worldwide.

Only then will the present age come to an end and Jesus will return.

And this gospel of the kingdom shall be preached in all the world for a witness unto all nations; and then shall the end come.
(Matthew 24:14 KJV)

This in turn means also:

4. From out of the Glory the harvest *takes place.* This means that a life in the Glory of God is never about it being only for yourself but always has a specific goal – the assignment from Jesus to once and for all bring the great commission to an end, and to bring in the full measure of the worldwide harvest into the "barns of God".

When I had this vision I was not yet aware that the Holy Spirit would instruct me shortly after to found a ministry with the name "Glory Harvest International" which would realize exactly this vision.

Since then we have experienced what far-reaching effects the Glory of God can have in a whole region or nation when it is received with child-like faith. For example, during our trip to Uganda in January 2015 with a five-member team from Glory Harvest International, we not only experienced mighty signs and miracles and salvations during our crusade services, conferences and pastors' meetings, but we were also able to experience how the natural and spiritual climate in a whole region changed permanently.

On the second day of a series of events in East Uganda during a pastors' meeting, we experienced a breakthrough of the Glory of God. Everything began to fill with the powerful presence of God, demons were cast out, signs and miracles happened and a great joy was set free.

It hadn't rained for 5 weeks in this usually very fruitful and green area which was a threatening situation for the rural population who lived solely from the yield of their fields and gardens.

After this glory breakthrough, we made our way to where the open-air crusade was to take place. We had hardly arrived when it started pouring buckets of rain for a half an hour. With great excitement the native population received this as a visible sign of God's blessing and the following open-air service was a powerful miracle and harvest evening with many healings and salvations. The people were so full of joy and enthusiasm about the demonstration of God's presence and power in their region that they danced until well into the night after we had left the field.

The following day the region was blessed with another downpour of rain – the dry season was at last over. And once again many healings, miracles and salvations took place.

At the end we laid hands personally on the local pastors ordaining them for their ministries so that they would come into a lasting spiritual relationship with us. A day later we drove to the next region.

And here, to the glory of God, is the summary of what we heard from East Uganda after our return to Germany:

The following report comes from Uganda about how things went after the team had left in January:

The pastors from the area in Eastern Uganda report that since the evangelistic meetings, teachings and pastors' seminars where the Glory of God broke through mightily, a genuine revival is taking place in the area:

In the previously "quiet" hosting church where there had been little supernatural manifestations of God, the Holy Spirit now falls regularly in a mighty way. People shake and scream under the amazingly powerful and very convicting presence of God. Many were saved and the supernatural work of the Holy Spirit is manifested in every respect in a mighty way.

People from everywhere are flocking into the church (whereas before they only came if they were in great need). The church building is now too small for the number of visitors that are crowding in for their meetings. The church has now become a hub for the mighty work of God in the region. At the same time the "competitive thinking" amongst the church pastors in the region has greatly declined and they are pulling together for this movement of God's love.

The testimony from a once mentally deranged woman who, during a crusade meeting with Pastor Georg, was supernaturally delivered and healed and is since then completely normal, has made a strong impression and attracted many former unbelievers. Meanwhile, for example, a gang of thieves came to Jesus who, until then, had made the streets unsafe. They are now coming to church.

In order to spread the revival that has begun, the involved pastors are now going to other places (e.g. to Kampala) and, on invitation, teach the local pastors so that the revival spreads further in the country. This means that within one week of our team being there God caused a spiritual shift which now continually spreads, step-by-step, under the leadership of the local leaders and pastors in Uganda.'

Is it not exciting to see how the Glory of God works? Completely independent of us human vessels it continues to turn a whole region upside down and brings in the harvest.

We – you and I – carry this Glory of God with us wherever we go – but the Glory, i.e. God Himself, does His work and brings in the harvest – worldwide!

SUMMARY

- The Glory of God leads us automatically into the harvest. It has ultimately been given to us for this purpose, to fulfill the Great Commission of the Father.

- We, as the Body of Christ, will be able to bring in the promised worldwide end-time harvest only out of the Glory of God.

- The Glory of God means the death of our old man but, at the same time, a heavenly filled new life in Godly fruitfulness.

PART III

YOUR JOURNEY INTO THE GLORY

14

"ALREADY" AND "NOT YET"

When we have completely taken in and believe the truth of the full Gospel according to the Bible (see previous chapters), then we know that we, *in the Spirit,* through Jesus, are already seated with Him in the realms of His Glory (Ephesians 2:6). The same glory that Jesus received from the Father is given to us and is uncompromisingly available to us at any time (John 17:22). We are *already a part of the new creation* (2 Corinthians 5:17) – even if the final takeover of the old creation (and therewith its complete renewal) through this new creation is still pending until the time of God's final judgment (see Revelations 20:11-22:5).

We are living in a kind of "interim era", also called the "Age of the Holy Spirit" wherein the new world is already becoming more and more real through the sons and daughters of God, but the final transformation of the entire currently existing world has not yet taken place. One could also say that Jesus Christ, after His resurrection, has already returned to the earth in the Spirit through the Holy Spirit in those who have received Him. Just His final return, which will be physically visible to all people, is still to come[18].

This means for us, who in the Spirit already belong to the new creation, that on the one hand we have to put up with a *visible* reality around us which

---

[18] To maintain that this second coming has already occurred is a classic heresy with which the Apostle Paul also had to deal with – see 2 Thessalonians 2:2

doesn't yet reflect heaven on earth, but, on the other hand, we have an *invisible* reality "within us" that *is* already heaven on earth.

In the spiritual realm everything is already accomplished – but not yet in the natural. It is our duty as children of God to increasingly penetrate the natural realm with the spiritual.

Our mission as children of God is to live out of *this inner spiritual reality* in order to increasingly transform the world around us into the likeness of this new creation – i.e. heaven on earth!

According to the Bible we can expect that the closer we get to the end of times, the return of Jesus and the final transformation of all things, and the more the Holy Spirit prepares the Bride of Christ for the coming of the Lord, the more the perceptible presence of the Glory of God and its visible impact in all aspects of life will increase.

The "not yet" in the natural will increasingly yield to the "already" which is at this point fully effective in the spiritual realm. Heaven is getting more and more real on this earth!

This is exactly the context in which your personal journey into the glory is now taking place …

The principle of transformation from the spirit into the natural applies to the world around us, as well as to our personal lives as "spirit-soul-body beings". The longer we walk this journey focusing on the Glory of God, the more our souls and our bodies are imbued and refashioned by this glory. This way we will reflect more and more visibly and perceptibly this invisible reality in all facets of our thinking, speech, emotion, ambition and radiance etc.

Subsequently, we will experience how also the world around us, our families, cities and nations are transformed even more from out of the glory into the original heavenly reality.

Some Christians may object and ask, "Doesn't the Bible say that in the end times there will be an increase of sin, catastrophes, famines, wars etc. How does that fit in with these statements?"

If you study Isaiah 60, a chapter I understand as being a prophetic preview of the movement of God's Glory in and through the sons during end times, you will realize that the Bible indeed sees both these "movements" as happening *simultaneously:* On the one hand (progressive) darkness covers this earth and all who are subject to the system of the prince of this world (Isaiah 60:2, and also in Jesus's end-times speech in Matthew 24:4-14). At the same time, on the other hand, the Glory of God accompanied with visible, perceptible and measurable effects in, on and through the sons of God will increase enormously, and masses of people who are presently still under the power of darkness will be pulled in and transformed by this Glory (Isaiah 60:1-9):

> *Arise, shine, for your light has come, and the glory of the LORD has risen upon you.* **See, darkness covers the earth and thick darkness is over the peoples, but the LORD rises upon you and his glory appears over you.** *Nations will come to your light, and kings to the brightness of your dawn. "Lift up your eyes and look about you: All assemble and come to you; your sons come from afar, and your daughters are carried on the hip. Then you will look and be radiant, your heart will throb and swell with joy; the wealth on the seas will be brought to you, to you the riches of the nations will come... "Who are these that fly along like clouds, like doves to their nests? Surely the islands look to me; in the lead are the ships of Tarshish, bringing your children from afar, with their silver and gold, to the honor of the LORD your God, the Holy One of Israel, for he has endowed you with splendor.*

This means that we will increasingly experience both growing darkness, a shaking (Hebrews 12:27), chaos in the world and, at the same time, an increase in Glory and godly transformation in and through the church of Jesus Christ of the end-times.

In times to come the darkness in the world and the glory in and on the sons of God will increase tremendously.

Jesus is not coming to fetch a wrinkled and weak bride but rather a *magnificent* – yes, a *glorified* bride who is actively spreading the Kingdom of

God and increasingly bringing heaven on earth all over the world, covering all aspects of life.

Confess right now: *In the Spirit, I keep my eyes on the Glory of God which infuses every pore of my being. It radiates more and more from every aspect of my life and thus transforms the whole world around me – from glory to even greater glory.*

15

FAITH AND HUNGER

So how do you actually keep on moving into, living in and through the Glory of God in the here and now?

Firstly, you need to take a hold of this new creation reality given to you by the Grace of God through faith, realizing that *it is already finished.* I am who the Word of God says that I am (a new creation, a son of God, a bearer of His Glory). *The spirit of the Lord is on me* (Luke 4:18). I have what the Word of God tells me I have *(...who has blessed us in the heavenly realms with every spiritual blessing in Christ.* Ephesians 1:3) and I can do what the Word of God says I can do –everything! (See Philippians 4:13). The Glory of God lives in me and penetrates every fiber of my being.

That is the spiritual reality in and through which you live (Galatians 5:16)! *It is here now!* Jesus has accomplished it once and for all – for us. There is nothing that can be added to His redemption work. If you only believe (meaning grasping it in your spirit), you will see the Glory of God, i.e. experience it continuously (John 11:40)!

Secondly, you need to be aware that your natural man (your soul and your body), as well as your environment, urgently needs transformation and always more transformation.

This consciousness (being aware), of what is not there yet, (outside of the spirit) creates in you an insatiable hunger for more of God, more of His Power, more of His Glory, more of His miracles, more of His nature and essence in your life and this hunger continually propels you forward!

The promises of Jesus are there for the hungry! Blessed are the poor in spirit (those who realize that they really need God), for theirs is the kingdom of heaven. Blessed are those who hunger and thirst for righteousness, for they will be filled. Matthew 5:3+6.

About 30 years ago I reached out to God for the first time. Since then I cannot remember more than a few days passing where I did not reach out for the things of God with a deep inner yearning and an almost desperate hunger!

Yes, there is this permanent deep yearning in your spirit for more of God (this is what Psalm 42:7 describes by "deep calls to deep"), an unconditional inner reaching out to God, which is not willing to let go until this deep hunger has been satisfied *("I will not let you go unless you bless me." Genesis 32:26).* This is what will take us into the deeper things of the Spirit. You could also say it catapults us into higher heavenly realms! This hunger slumbers in the spirit of every born-again child of God. All you have to do is make room for it, awaken or kindle it. Sometimes I consciously speak to this hunger when I realize my soul has been inclined to complacency for a while!

You can literally "hunger for hunger" because you know there is no progress without hunger!

In all of this, it is vitally important that spiritual *hunger* and *faith* in the completed work of Jesus Christ on the Cross always go hand in hand – as Matthew 21:22 aptly puts it: *If you* **believe***, you will receive* **whatever** *you ask for in prayer.*

This basically means, when this deep inner hunger is joined with the promises of God through faith, you receive in that precise moment this new dimension for which you have stretched out for: *Therefore I tell you, whatever you ask for in prayer, believe that you* **have received** *it, and it will be yours* (Mark 11:24).

Countless times I have experienced that as I reached out in faith from the depth of my spirit, only a few days, hours, or sometimes even minutes later, it became manifest for me! And you will experience this as well when you learn to kindle your spiritual hunger, linking it to God's promises in faith.

Hunger without faith eventually leads to frustration. Faith without hunger eventually leads to complacency and half-heartedness. However, hunger paired with faith invariably receives something new constantly – and indeed straightaway!

You will not "earn" any points by stretching out in hunger towards God. It is also not an "achievement" on your part "proving" something to God (this kind of attitude has its roots in a religious spirit and will only leave you exhausted and frustrated).

However, hunger, coupled with the faith of standing on God's Word immediately, receives always new, and more and more!

For this reason, on the one hand, it is important for your spiritual life that you hungrily keep on reaching for more of God's Glory. On the other hand, you need to believe that Jesus has already provided, in the spiritual realm, what you are yearning for so that all you have to do is take it!

16

THE CROSS AND THE GLORY

Even though our inner, spiritual man has been completely made new in the image of Jesus Christ when we were born again (Ephesians 2:10; Colossians 2:10), our souls and our bodies still need renewal (see Romans 12:1-2; 1Thessalonians 5:23).

This renewal does not follow specific human patterns, and it definitely is no outward Christian "behavior therapy".

It happens through the supernatural working of the Cross and the Resurrection *Glory* of Jesus Christ in our lives!

This means that we are being transformed by contemplating the Lord's glory, sitting at the right hand of God (2 Corinthians 3:18[19]. By constantly focusing on what is above (Colossians 3:1-4) we are being transformed into that same likeness – which is the image of Jesus and, in conclusion, the image of the Father Himself. Our transformation begins with the spirit and also embraces our soul and body in the process!

If you simply keep your eyes consistently on this Glory – which is ultimately God Himself – nothing and no one can stop your transformation and

---

[19] *And we all, who with unveiled faces contemplate the Lord's glory, are being transformed into his image with ever-increasing glory, which comes from the Lord, who is the Spirit.*

"glorification process"! And, at the same time, the power of "death" from the cross of Jesus is mysteriously and constantly working in us!

We are being transformed by focusing on the Glory of God and by the mysterious power of the cross, to which our flesh has been nailed through faith!

The Bible says that all life "according to the flesh" is diametrically contrary to the Spirit of God and consequently also to His Glory in our lives:

Those who live according to the flesh have their minds set on what the flesh desires; but those who live in accordance with the Spirit have their minds set on what the Spirit desires. The mind governed by the flesh is death, but the mind governed by the Spirit is life and peace. The mind governed by the flesh is hostile to God; it does not submit to God's law, nor can it do so. Those who are in the realm of the flesh cannot please God. You, however, are not in the realm of the flesh but are in the realm of the Spirit, if indeed the Spirit of God lives in you. (Romans 8:5-9).

This human "flesh", which basically means a life governed by our senses, fears, outward circumstances, is never "treatable". From a biblical point of view there is only one "cure" for the flesh and that is crucifixion!

Those who belong to Christ Jesus have crucified the flesh with its passions and desires. (Galatians 5:24)

Paul describes the result as follows: *I have been crucified with Christ and I no longer live, but Christ lives in me* (Galatians 2:20).

Through the completed work of Jesus Christ on the cross and our faith in it, our flesh has already been crucified which means it is dead!

We should never live in a consciousness of still being "in the flesh" when Jesus is inside of us because it would then mean that we do not believe that Jesus has already accomplished all for us on the cross!

No, the flesh has already been crucified, and we therefore need to, once and for all, consider it completely dead (there is probably no method more deadly than crucifixion!). In Christ we *have* already put off our old self which is corrupted by its deceitful desires (Ephesians 4:22). Believing anything else is not in accordance with the Gospel and would imply that we believe the new creation that Jesus accomplished through His resurrection work is incomplete!

However, as long as our outer man (meaning soul and body) still resides in this world ruled by the devil, our belief that our flesh is ultimately dead will frequently be tested by the devil!

This means that he will try to create circumstances, influence people or also reactivate past thought-patterns and emotional structures in order to "take our flesh off the cross or out of the grave". In other words, he will (subjectively!) put pressure on us to dare us to react "according to the flesh"! He wants to steal our belief that the flesh is already crucified and that there actually is no reason to return to it! For this purpose he uses certain challenges in order to mislead us to "revive" the flesh again.

Nowhere in the Bible does it say that we as Christians will not have troubles any more. However, the Bible does show us an unimpeachable way to walk through every one of these trials, mysteriously being strengthened and transformed into the image of His Glory!

Meditate on **2 Corinthians 4:17-18**: For our light and momentary troubles are achieving for us an eternal glory that far outweighs them all. So we fix our eyes not on what is seen, but what is unseen, since what is seen is temporary, but what is unseen is eternal.

What does this mean?

Quite simple: When outward hardships attack us (persecution, spiritual, emotional, physical or material attacks) we must decide to either react with unbelief thus resuscitating our actually crucified and dead flesh, or we immediately turn our focus away from those hardships and to the reality of the Glory of God i.e. to heaven, to God Himself – and see what He will do or, in some cases, what He sometimes will refrain from doing!

If we opt for the latter (which Paul urges us to do here), in that specific moment we declare to the seen and the unseen world that we truly consider the natural man as dead according to Galatians 2:20 and Galatians 5:24. We ignore our natural man (which includes any current suffering,—wailing or complaining) and, through faith, declare it irrelevant (since it has already been crucified). We refuse to "react" to outward hardships "in the flesh".

If we continue to do this in faith with a determined spirit in the face of affliction, we truly will be mysteriously changed spiritually. A greater "weight" of glory descends onto our lives which will, in retrospect, leave only a light and passing memory of any hardship we have gone through.

Being spiritual personalities hungry for more of the Glory of God, we can ultimately rejoice consciously (and especially!) when we are going through afflictions – because an even greater weight of the Glory of God is about to come into our lives!

Through all of this, the sayings of Jesus and Paul become easy to understand and without alternative as they exhort us to rejoice constantly (and even aggressively) in the most challenging hardships. See for instance Luke 6:22-23: *Blessed are you when people hate you, when they exclude you and insult you and reject your name as evil, because of the Son of Man. Rejoice in that day and leap for joy, because great is your reward in heaven.*

Or Philippians 4:4: *Rejoice in the Lord always,* or Philippians 2:17-18 etc…

Because, if the devil does not manage to steal your joy in the face of outward hardships, he will not be able to pull you down to the level of the flesh. And then nothing will stand in the way of your next "promotion" into a greater dimension of the Glory of God!

Rejoice "aggressively" even in the face of outward hardships and you will never leave the realm of faith in which you believe your flesh is dead and you are living in the glory!

This is foolishness for the human mind, but for us a vital key on our journey into glory!

Therefore, rejoice, if necessary *aggressively* – and allow the power of the cross of Jesus to work on your natural man. In this way, the natural man will learn to live crucified permanently while living according to the Spirit (Galatians 5:16) and not according to the flesh, thus going from one glory to the next even greater glory!

17

"FALLING INTO" THE GLORY

The natural man would always like to have a to-do-list or plan that he could follow in order to reach a certain goal.

He wants to work hard for something, and the concept of "by grace through faith" (Ephesians 2:8) is completely foreign to him.

The soul of man wrestles and fights for what is important to him (e.g. like maybe, after reading this book, for a life in the Glory of God). The spiritually renewed man, however, has progressively learned to just let himself "fall into" the grace of God in faith.

So when someone asks me, "How did you manage to get into this supernatural dimension of glory?" I like to answer them, "I have somehow *fallen* into it rather than *managed to get* into it."

If you really want to experience the Glory of God in your life you will have to come to the point over and over again where you just let go of all your spiritual "disciplines" like worship, prayer, study of the Word, hungering after the reality of God (as important as they all are), and by mere trust just let yourself "fall into" what God has already prepared for you.

That's how I have had some of my most powerful encounters and revelations from God – while I was lying totally relaxed on my sofa, or on the floor, being aware of God's presence. I just "passively" exposed myself to His presence.

More often than not, I consciously make my soul let go of everything that is still occupying it. This includes all circumstances, situations, people and distractions etc. that still influence it. I do this by just consciously going "higher" in my spirit. Just think about the command of the angel to John in Revelation 4:1 *"Come up here!"*

You do not "work" yourself into the Glory of God, you "fall into" it.

I go higher than the questions, higher than the problems, higher than the circumstances, higher than the people who previously pulled on my soul, higher than everything else in this world.

I empty my soul of all other "impressions", so that it becomes free to being only "impressed" by God Himself and His Glory. I then reach a point where I stop fighting, stop hungering or stop "having" faith (at least consciously), and I trustfully let my soul fall into the loving arms of its creator. And then suddenly I am in God's Glory and experience it, either tangibly, visibly or audibly – depending on what God wants to do with me.

Sometimes He is just there and lets me sense His presence, sometimes He shows me a little vision, sometimes He speaks to my heart, and sometimes He allows me to enter into more spectacular experiences like trances or other things – just as the Holy Spirit wills. And He definitely wants to give this to you as much as He wants to give it to me.

THE FATHER'S FAVORITES

I believe it is very important that we come to the point where the fact that we are God's beloved children (yes, His favorites!) becomes an unconscious faith reality in our lives. This reality should go deeper than our mind and our consciousness, and we should be able to fall fearlessly into it at any time.

God is good and He has only good things in mind for you and me.

He won't give you a snake if you ask Him for a fish, and He won't give you a scorpion if you ask Him for an egg (Luke 11:11-13).

Some people say that God has no favorites. I am telling you that God only has favorites. Each one of His children is His favorite child.

Consequently, if anywhere in the world any son of God can experience a certain blessing, a certain grace, a certain dimension of the Glory of God then I (and you!) can have it also. No one is more a favorite of God than you and me!

We need to be more "John-conscious" in the Body of Christ. John simply knew that he was "the disciple whom Jesus loved" and he even had the guts to mention this repeatedly in his Gospel. Why do you think John was the only disciple who stayed close to Jesus until the end at the cross? I personally believe that this fact is strongly connected to his own perception of being "the favorite".

Peter had a completely different take on this at first, a way of thinking that made him compare by asking, "Lord, what about him?" (John 21:21). His mindset made him envious of John.

From the Lord's point of view he could actually have had the same attitude as John – because there is no rivalry amongst God's favorites. Rivalry and envy only exist among those feeling inferior who believe that God gave them the "short end of the stick". In the heart of God, however, everybody has the same place – all are His favorites. Those who are aware of this will never feel threatened by another son of God, nor will they feel inferior just because somebody else has "more of God" than they do. No, they would rather say, "I can have the same as well. I just pull it into my life because I am also the Father's favorite."

You don't need to compare yourself with others because you know: I am the absolute favorite of my Father.

Others may believe whatever they want about themselves (hopefully that they are the favorite), but I myself believe that I am definitely the favorite of my Father. In this awareness, in this assurance, you can let go of everything else and let yourself fall into God. That's how you get overwhelmed by His wonderful, mighty Glory.

In order to create a lasting foundation for experiencing the Glory of God, the key ingredient to your spiritual life is not your discipline – as important as this is in order to continually live effectively for God. It is also not your spiritual "performance" in worship, prayer, bible reading etc. – as important as these things are as well.

No, the single most important thing out of which all the other things come is your trust in the love of your Father! Your consciousness of being His favorite, His special "darling" in whose company He has endless delight and to whom He thus so gladly wants to reveal all of His Glory, and all that defines Him.

While I was writing this book, Jesus once asked me during a time of prayer, *What do you believe was the most important goal of my ministry on this earth?* And He immediately answered the question Himself and said, *To reveal to mankind how much the Father loves them!* Go to the recordings of the Gospels and you will find that this motive is found again and again between the lines.

This revelation of the love of the Father will automatically lead you to the point where you *want* to take more and more time to rest in Him, to let go of your thoughts and distractions and to exclusively focus on Him. Just you and Him, all alone…

And so, God and man unite, heaven touches earth and in a mysterious way this world is being filled and changed by this supernatural reality!

Very often, during these sometimes lengthy times while I am exposing myself like a child to the Glory of my Father, I afterwards realize, without having thought about it, that a new empowerment, a new clarity, fresh revelation and new, transforming and miracle working power has taken effect in my life and ministry – *just like that.*

I therefore encourage you to regularly "expose" yourself to the Glory of God in your life, to let yourself "fall into it" and to just "receive from it" by finding rest from your own works. Hebrews 4:9-11 *There remains, then, a Sabbath-rest for the people of God; for anyone who enters God's rest also rests from their works, just as God did from his. Let us, therefore, make every effort to enter that rest…!*

It actually is so much easier than our mind sometimes would have us believe!

So, right now you can start with your journey…

18

MAKING THE GLORY OF GOD

THE PRIORITY OF YOUR LIFE

It was a very important day in my life when I decided to make the Glory of God my first and highest priority for the rest of my life (besides God Himself of course, although both really are one).

It is my whole passion to see the Glory of God and all the supernatural that is included therein continually manifested in my own life, as well as in the life of the church of Jesus Christ.

And I know that only with this determination we will really *continually* experience the Glory of God in our midst.

As Christians, and as the church, we are a temple of the Holy Spirit. This means when people look at us or come to our meetings they should have an encounter with the Glory of God (consciously or unconsciously).

The Glory of God is our destiny. We come from it, we live in it and we return to it. Even if some people might consider us a little "crazy" or "strange" we should still be known for one thing, and that is that we know God and that He is working in our midst. If people need healing or a miracle, their first thought should be the church – and not some "spiritual healer", shaman or New Ager!

The devil has personally offered me many alternatives as to what I should give my life for (even as a Christian). As you can read in the first chapter I have definitely swayed again and again during my first years as a Christian, but meanwhile I (and all those who walk this path with me) have made our ultimate decision in that there won't be a change of topic anymore. God's supernatural and revival-related workings, the pulling down of heaven to this earth, the manifestation of His Glory in the midst of His people and in the midst of this world – that is our mission and that is our destiny.

This decision makes it very easy now, from the get-go, to identify all other "ideas" as being a diversion and to rule out many types of pseudo-leadings.

Like the people of Israel on their journey we are also solely led by the pillar of God's Glory (Exodus 40:34-38). When the pillar rests we rest, when the pillar lifts we set out with it – wherever it goes, that's where we go.

Everything that intensifies the Glory in our life and ministry is what we want and anything else, even if it looks good or even promises more visible (short-term) success, we don't want.

We know that the most successful and victorious way for us in the long run is not some concept of church development, not a method to win people and not some well devised and correct biblical theology (as good as all these things are) – but rather His vibrant Glory in our midst.

When you have made a clear decision that living in and out of the Glory of God is the absolute and eternal priority for your life, then everything in your spiritual life becomes much easier.

When being led by the Glory it is very easy to discern what comes from God and what does not, which spirit is from Him and which spirit is from the other side. This is because the Holy Spirit always makes room for the Glory and presence of God in the midst of His people, and He does everything to boost it. Other spirits of religious or worldly nature always do the opposite. They try to persuade the people of God that it is quite okay to stay on a "lower" level of spiritual life. Yes, they even warn you of "wanting more", and they create whole theologies around the theory that nowadays God doesn't want to work as He used to, or that we don't really "need" His move – at least in this "extreme form" – in order to reach the world.

Well, they can say whatever they like. People may fight this move of God however they want. My decision stands to go with the Glory of God and to unconditionally follow the cloud and pillar of fire for the rest of my life.

What about you?

Once you have made this irreversible decision, a lot of things in your spiritual life will become much "easier"!

PART IV

THE TANGIBLE AND PERCEPTIBLE EFFECTS OF LIVING IN THE GLORY

19

COMING ALIVE AGAIN IN THE

GLORY

If the Glory of God is the original habitat that God intended for mankind, and Jesus again provided us with free access into that realm through His redemptive work, the first consequence of getting hold of this realm by faith and learning to live in it consistently will automatically be that our whole being – spirit, soul and body, will be endlessly reinvigorated.

Like a fish that finds its way back into the water after having been out of it for some time, so will we, in the literal sense of the word, "breathe in" new life in this atmosphere of the manifest Glory of God.

The devil is the dominant spirit in the air over "this world" (Ephesians 2:2).

This means as long as we dwell in the *spiritual* realm of "this world", we will have all kinds of fears and troubles in our souls (John 16:33). However, the moment we enter into the spiritual realm of the Glory of God, all fear and trouble just falls away from us and everything in us becomes boundlessly light, joyful and free.

We have so often heard or received written testimonies where somebody said, "I came to your service completely shattered, seemingly at the end of my rope. I was discouraged, full of fear and sorrow and then suddenly during the service all of that just fell off me, and now my soul has a whole new perspective!"

That's a sign that the Glory of God was present in a meeting in one way or another.

In the atmosphere of Glory "everything" can change for you in the twinkling of an eye.

Often you don't really know what actually happened but somehow the *atmosphere* that you were in completely changed the condition of your soul. Sometimes it was a specific word that served as a decisive key to unlock the lock of your inner man, sometimes it was the worship. But very often, afterwards, you don't know what it really was. There is only one thing you know, somehow you have lost those formerly dominant strange, black thoughts and feelings pulling you down, now everything is completely different, those thoughts and feelings are not part of you any longer.

I would explain it this way: Your soul simply changed its "dwelling place" while you were still seated on the same chair or standing in the same place.

Your spirit (with the Holy Spirit inside) has been activated through Jesus and has drawn your body and soul into that very same dimension in which the newly created spirit is already permanently dwelling, i.e. into the Glory of God.

The following testimony from a lady that had simply listened to one of our messages illustrates this:

Dear Pastor Georg Karl,

I have discovered that I can download messages from your website…

While listening to one of the messages Jesus suddenly ran towards me and showed me how much He loved me. This happened in the twinkling of an eye and I don't know how to describe it.

I suddenly saw clearly that I sometimes had to fight with severe depression but had become so used to it that I didn't really recognize the problem as such anymore.

> Within a second all of this left me and I can now enjoy my life because I now see that He really loves me...C.B.

Can you see that? It's not the external place that decides on how you feel and what you experience – it is the spiritual realm. Are you living in the realm of darkness or in the realm of the Son He loves (Colossians 1:13)? By nature you have been under the dominion of the devil – but through the finished redemptive work of God you have entered into the dominion of the Son of His love which is the dominion of God's Glory. This is the realm for which you have actually, always been predestined for from the beginning of your creation.

THE SIGNIFICANCE OF YOUR WORDS

Faith in this reality is primarily exercised through words: *Consequently, faith comes from hearing the message, and the message is heard through the word of Christ.* (Romans 10:17)

This means that if you and others around you, e.g. in a service, speak out words of faith in the full Gospel and thank God for His manifest Glory based on His revealed word, focusing consciously on things above, you then enter into the atmosphere of God's Glory, and in the spirit you also create this same atmosphere all around you. For example, we might say, "Thank you Father for your Glory in us and in our midst. Thank you that through Jesus we live in this dimension and have our dwelling place in heaven." Out of His glory we then release an atmosphere in the whole room which is "pregnant" with divine power, peace, joy, health, miracles, the presence of angels etc.

By your words you create the "atmosphere" in which you live.

The result is a deep inner reviving and recovering of soul and body. As people learn to live in this realm more and more constantly then the effects become more permanent and deeper.

So, if possible, start using your mouth today to build a foundation for an atmosphere of glory in your personal life and surroundings by speaking words of faith.

As an illustration for the tangible consequences of this atmosphere, here is another testimony from a lady which she wrote seven months after her salvation:

Hello Pastor Georg and Irina,

I have now been attending your church for about 7 months and I can't imagine living my life any more without the Word and the messages on Thursdays and Sundays. What is even greater, I am eternally thankful for the number of little miracles happening constantly.

In the beginning I cried a lot and I didn't understand many things, but as you always say, Georg, it is a journey and it is the staying on track that continuously helps you on. Meanwhile, my heart has been healed of pain, sadness and anger, frustration and anxiety, and I am now happily looking forward to the time ahead of me. There are miracles happening in my everyday life which would have been unthinkable 7 months ago.

Just two little examples: For 6 years I hadn't had any contact with my parents. When my son died I gave permission to donate his organs so my father always said that I had killed his grandson. It's over with now and, thank God, today I have a normal and even loving and peaceful relationship with my parents. My Mom came to the healing service in October and since then she is at such deep peace with herself and with other people like I have never seen before in her. She had diabetes for 20 years and that is now also gone.

Miracle number two: After not having had a day off for 6 years, this year I am able to go on holiday again. My finances are getting better and better! I have a calmness and a peace within me that I can't describe with words. My heart has been healed, I have no more fear but instead a deep joy growing on the inside of me. From the bottom of my heart I am so thankful for EVERYTHING.

U.K.

THE SIGNIFICANCE OF THE "ATMOSPHERE"

In a worldly "atmosphere" our soul and our bodies would ultimately take on the ways of the world which is "passing away" (1 Corinthians 7:31; 1 John 2:17).

This means that outward and inward decay are inevitable.

Moreover, in a worldly "atmosphere" we would be led, without noticing it, step-by-step into doing bad things (=sin)– while, at the same time, being convinced to have the best motives (Ephesians 2:2-3).

A "religious" atmosphere is also not an alternative for the Glory of God. The essence of every kind of religion (even if it is camouflaged as "Christian"), is to encourage people to please God out of their own strength and works in order to receive acceptance and blessings from Him. However, this will in all eternity simply be impossible, as everything that God has for us as humans has to be received by grace through faith (Ephesians 2:8). As I said before, you don't work for the Glory of God, but rather "fall" into it by faith.

The atmosphere in which you live determines in which direction your life will change.

People or churches that live under a religious spirit will always be recognized by their joylessness, the strain and pressure on them, as well as the harshness towards those who are not as "good" as they are.

There will always be something like a "blanket" lying on a meeting that is under the control of a religious spirit. Under this blanket all kinds of depressive, fearful and legalistic spirits can exist without being disturbed.

What is more, the religious spirit will always be the spirit that fights against the true manifestation of the Glory of God in the strongest, fiercest and most relentless way – even more radically than the spirit of the world.

The life of Jesus perfectly illustrates this as He, of course, has set the standard for this confrontation of the spirits (you could also call it, "the confrontation of the atmospheres").

Nobody has fought Jesus as hard, maliciously and deviously as the "orthodox" teachers of the law and the Pharisees in whom the religious spirit manifested in its purest form.

For this reason it is often even more destroying and harmful to move in a religious atmosphere than in a worldly one. If the version of religion that we are confronted with is very close to biblical truth it is especially enticing to us as sons and daughters of God who wholeheartedly want to follow Jesus and obey His word. The danger to come under that spirit is then even greater.

It is therefore utterly important that we as Christians learn to really discern the spirits (and this very much includes the "atmospheres"), see Hebrews 5:14. As already mentioned in the first part of this book, during the beginning of my Christian walk my own incapability of discerning the spirits and the atmospheres – or not sticking with that what I already felt deep within me – caused me again and again to walk many circles in the desert, and gave me lots of insecurities, depression and anxiety. This was the case although I believed in Jesus and His Word. However, God would really like to spare us this. So, be very aware of the "atmospheres" which you open yourself up to.

FELLOWSHIP

Everything really starts out with us as Christians finding a fellowship with other believers who have made living in the full reality of the Gospel, i.e. in His Glory, their ultimate goal.

Another kind of fellowship doesn't really qualify as a source of inspiration and life as we would then go back to being under atmospheres, blankets and eventually come under "spirits" that make it very hard for us to maintain the reality of the Glory of God in our personal life.

You need fellowship with other Christians who have made a decision for a life in the atmosphere of God's Glory.

Since the promise of the manifest presence of Jesus in fullness ultimately rests on the fellowship of His Body, we also can't get very far *without* being part of a fellowship of believers (Matthew 18:20; Hebrews 10:22-25).

The perfect plan of God is rather to let us grow *in the fellowship* of God's family so that we can cultivate an atmosphere of Glory 24/7 *in our own everyday lives*.

Our spiritual discernment won't ever really grow if we move around in this world all alone without the fellowship of other sons and daughters of God who have started out on the same journey into glory, because *"iron sharpens iron"* (Proverbs 27:17).

Many Christians who have no church fellowship run around and think they can judge everything and everybody but truly understand nothing:

"The man who thinks he knows something does not yet know as he ought to know." (1 Corinthians 8:2). And one verse earlier it says: "Knowledge puffs up, but love builds up."

Love is truly lived out in *fellowship!*

20

INWARD AND OUTWARD TRANSFORMATION THROUGH THE GLORY OF GOD

The inward sigh of relief and the becoming whole in the Glory of God that I have already mentioned will automatically impact your entire life because you have now arrived as a triune being with a spirit, soul and body in the habitat which actually has originally been ordained for you by God's order of creation!

Sometimes, and, indeed, with increased regularity we are privileged to experience these effects becoming tangible and visible immediately and spontaneously. That's what we then call a "miracle". "Healing miracles" in the physical realm, "deliverance miracles" in the realm of the soul or "financial miracles" in the material realm and so on.

At the same time deep transformation can of course also be experienced as a process over an extended period of time while we are still learning to permanently live in the Glory. That's what we call "gradual healing", "step-by-step restoration" or "renewal".

The outward visible signs of this mighty new energy flooding your entire inward and outward being in the realm of the Glory includes classic healings like from cancer, diabetes, arthritis, movement restrictions etc., creative miracles like the disappearance or transformation of metal implants in the body, the creation of new body parts or organs etc., as well as signs and wonders that reverse age-related conditions, such as the dissolving of age spots or scar tissue, supernatural weight loss or even the spontaneous disappearance of wrinkles etc. – all in the atmosphere of the Glory!

The *inner* transformation of the personality taking place through the Glory of God certainly is equally important though.

Whoever spends time in a certain atmosphere for an extended period will sooner or later reflect the expression of this very atmosphere.

THE EXPRESSION OF THE GLORY ATMOSPHERE

Now what is the expression of the atmosphere of God's Glory? Let's read 1 Chronicles 16:27: *Splendor and majesty are before him; strength and joy in his dwelling place.*

This means you can't stay continuously in the direct radiance of God without reflecting joy, power, excellence and dignity!

Outside the Glory of God there is joylessness, powerlessness, inferiority and false humility but we who focus on the Glory are being transformed into the image of this same Glory (2 Corinthians 3:18)!

A) JOY

In your presence there is fullness of joy (Psalm 16:11 ESV).

God is obviously a God of joy!

A Christian who doesn't like to be in an atmosphere of overflowing joy will encounter a culture shock when arriving in heaven one day!

Hebrews 1:9 states about Jesus, that he was...*anointed with the oil of gladness beyond his companions* (ESV). So, the image some of the older Jesus-movies convey of His personality might not be quite accurate...

In God there is nothing heavy, burdening or even oppressing. On the contrary an essential aspect of the atmosphere of heaven is joy as well as a spiritual ease and freedom (*where the spirit of the Lord is, there is freedom!* 2 Corinthians 3:17).

Even if the Glory of God sometimes manifests in a very convicting, profound or powerfully challenging way – the joy of the Lord is never far off and the overall atmosphere always is upbuilding, uplifting, prickling and strengthening!

Nehemiah 8:10 declares: *For the joy of the Lord is your strength / refuge / strong tower.*

This means in the long run it would be very difficult to lead a powerful, effective Christian life without continuously experiencing the joy of the Lord, and specifically choosing to be surrounded by an atmosphere of joy!

The joy of the Lord is one of the sharpest weapons against the devil and, because Jesus lives in you, you can release it out of your innermost being at any time!

Some Christians and churches are afraid of too much joy. They either have a totally wrong perception of God or they are embarrassed by the "Joy of the Lord". Maybe they also fear to lose their dignity or their self-control, or they might not have yet learned to cast their circumstances and burdens upon Jesus as 1 Peter 5:7 advises us to do. In some cases they even find some kind of satisfaction in showing off their own "burdensomeness".

Let's have a look at Philippians: Here we see Paul, probably writing from the prison in Rome to the Philippians, never getting tired of exhorting them to rejoice in the Lord "always" (Philippians 4:4; 3:1; 2:17-18).

If we can trust the descriptions of Roman prisons at that time, he probably all the while stood in a tiny, dark cell without any light, populated with rats and vermin. Furthermore, the latrine canal was located directly under his feet. On top of it all, Paul also had to constantly reckon with being called out for execution at any moment!

If there has ever been anyone who has had every reason to hang his head then Paul is the one! However, exactly this Paul encourages the Philippians in nearly every chapter of his letter to just keep on rejoicing, even if he himself should die a martyr's death (Philippians 2:17-18)!

I don't believe that real joy coming from the inside is at all possible for a human in the natural who finds himself in a situation like Paul's.

For this, an assuredness of something higher was necessary, the certainty of the presence of God, i.e. the reality of God's Glory in Paul's heart!

In the same way we, as sons of God, should constantly make the decision for the joy of the Lord, believing in this reality that is deep within us, thereby going against other spirits like oppression, fear, worry or depression.

The Bible clearly states that these rivers of overflowing living water (i.e. also of His joy) are already in us through Jesus, and they just have to be released in faith (John 7:38 *Whoever believes in me, as the Scripture has said, streams of living water will flow from within him.*)

This means we err as new creations in Christ if we suppose that the joy of the Lord always has to come supernaturally "upon us".

There are, of course, special anointings that release joy and laughter. However, apart from this, we as Christians have this source of joy – Jesus Himself – within us, and we just have to activate it and let it flow.

If we were dependent only on certain anointings, then a consistent walk in joy, especially in difficult situations, would be hardly possible for us!

No, the joy of the Lord is already *within us* and it is one of the most powerful weapons against the devil! At the same time joy is a part of the Glory of God. Even a small outbreak of joy can put a whole regiment of demons to flight in one second, and transform us from feeling like an "empty", "oppressed" and "exhausted" vessel to an overwhelmingly overflowing vessel of the power of God!

We cannot separate a life in the Glory of God from a life in and out of the joy of the Lord.

Here's a little testimony to illustrate the effectiveness of joy:

Dear Georg,

at the beginning of March I felt intense pain in the left side of my chest. When the skin started to turn red I consulted a physician. He diagnosed shingles which meant another 2 weeks of intense pain, followed by a long period of the pain only slowly decreasing. I refused to accept this course of the illness, and waited for help from my heavenly daddy. A week later, whilst on a long drive, I listened to the sermon entitled "Rivers of New Wine". Towards the end you "diagnosed" my current spiritual condition as 'the devil first robbed your health and now keeps you busy with thoughts about why you lost it!' The therapy was simply, 'Let yourself be filled with New Wine and rejoice in the Lord always, because the joy of the Lord is your strength!' The very next morning my pain was completely gone! I didn't need any more medication! The shingles had been stopped by the joy of the Lord! Hallelujah! Greetings from I.B.

Once God spoke clearly to me personally and said to me, "You are my happy preacher!"

Back then I surely wasn't an all-time "happy preacher", since I hadn't yet really, fully grasped the significance of the joy of the Lord for my spiritual life. However, I accepted this statement from God as an obligation and challenge. So, since then, I am "striving" to stay filled with heavenly joy as much as possible! It seems that my wife is especially thrilled about this commitment…

We are almost "obliged" to be joyful as Christians who believe in the finished atonement of Jesus!

In my opinion, the lack of joy and spiritual freedom in the life of many Christians and Christian gatherings and churches is a main hindrance for the sons of God living a victorious life. The manifestation of the Glory of God will however fundamentally change this!

There is no way of dwelling constantly in the Glory of God without being filled with new waves of joy. The ever new bubbling-over with joy is a significant part of the everyday-life of a Christian!

Let us therefore – right now – release the joy of God from our innermost being...whoohoo!

BECOMING LIKE CHILDREN

Jesus says in Matthew 18:3: I tell you the truth, unless you change and become like little children, you will never enter the kingdom of heaven.

You could also put it this way: without a childlike heart, you cannot experience the Glory of God in a permanent way!

Usually kids rejoice more easily than so-called "adults". They don't care as much about their countenance. They don't necessarily feel embarrassed when they are, from time to time, overcome with great joy. According to a study, kids laugh on average 400 times per day, whereas adults average just 15 times!

Children are open-minded, fully trusting, able to let go and accept and believe exactly what they are told.

As their intellectual capacities haven't yet developed that far they are not so much in danger of being dominated by them and so they act rather intuitively.

Jesus puts all of this before us as exemplary for ourselves!

At the same time do not mix "childlikeness" with "childishness". The latter just means "being immature" or "acting dumb and foolish"... Sometimes, however, the one is hardly distinguishable from the other when it comes to the things of God!

Only with a childlike heart can we really distinguish the divine from the carnal, and only with a childlike heart can we permanently host the Glory of God!

We definitely cannot evaluate from the outward behavior or appearance whether someone is childish/immature or childlike/godly.

A good example is portrayed by King David in 2 Samuel 6:12-23. Here David, while bringing up the Ark of the Covenant (i.e. the manifest presence of God under the old covenant), danced before the Lord with all his might wearing just a linen ephod – and this in full view of all the people! Evaluated from a natural, human point of view (like that of his wife Michal), that dance certainly looked rather "childish" and in the eyes of many people it was contradictory to David's dignity as king. The reason for this behavior was David's passionate heart for God, which couldn't care less about what people think. He simply thought that God deemed worthy his extreme – maybe even scandalous – way of expressing his joy!

"Man looks at the outward appearance, but the Lord looks at the heart." 1 Samuel 16:7

We ought to keep this statement continually in mind together with the fate of Michal[20], and we should be very careful to not be quick to judge anything. Even if some things might be uncomfortable to our flesh, this does not necessarily mean that they are not of God!

God told me once, "I want you to rejoice to the point of personal humiliation!" Several times I was so taken over by God that I did things (or rather let them happen), which in fact were totally embarrassing for me – knowing however that it was God working in and through me all along the line.

Your flesh can also be offended by a person close to you (e.g. your spouse) "manifesting" intensely under the power and Glory of God – but this also doesn't prove the manifestation itself is not of God.

So, time and again, simply let go and let the people around you be free – by doing this, your own heart will become pure and free!

MANIFESTATIONS

Talking about physical manifestations in churches where the Glory of God is operating with outbursts of uncontrollable joy, I dare to say that, based on the manifestations themselves, it is pointless to try and discern whether God is at work in a meeting or not.

---

[20]After rebuking David for his childlike dance of joy before the Lord, Michal remained barren for the rest of her life.

This is because manifestations are simply nothing but the *reactions of a specific human being* to the spiritual presence in a room. The *reactions* of a person can be demonic or carnal even if the *presence* in a room is pure glory, i.e. God (which can only be discerned in the Spirit). In the gospels we find demons screaming or certain people making very carnal statements –right in the presence of Jesus!

People's "manifestations" are just reactions to the spiritual atmosphere in a room!

If at all, you have to discern whether a demon or a carnal reaction to the Glory is manifesting *at a certain moment through a certain person* – and this is, of course, only possible by the supernatural gift of discernment, and not by our "feelings". The same manifestations after all can also be the experience of a healing or deliverance taking place, or maybe the person is enjoying the joy of the Lord and His electric presence!

As long as we are not in charge of a meeting we should not take much notice (or rather not at all!) of the people around us, but rather focus on God. Reach out to encounter Him yourself, instead of judging others, or even the whole congregation, concerning their being spiritual or of the flesh!

Where the spirit of the Lord is, there is freedom! So, there is indeed freedom for every one of God's sons and daughters to encounter God in the way that is right for them! If we want God's presence and Glory to feel at home continuously in our midst we shouldn't give attention to spirits of control and so become people pleasers in our churches.

Because little children are normally free of such controlling spirits and manlike or religious compulsions, Jesus presents them as a role model and encourages us to change and to become like them.

Controlling and critical spirits hinder the working of the Holy Spirit!

Sometimes in meetings I give the following criteria for the discernment of spirits (touched with a bit of humor): If you see someone sitting in the service with crossed arms and a grim or angry look on his face, you can assume that this person is presently *in the flesh*! Everything else you should leave up to God and the leaders He has appointed over the meeting and just relax. I believe most of us could very well use an extra serving of that ease…

It surely is spiritually and biblically safe to say that a lively, over-brimming, effortless joy coming out of the innermost being, accompanied by a childlike readiness to do unusual things or let them happen when the Holy Spirit leads, is undoubtedly a sign of a personality transformed by the Glory of God!

Such personalities around us can challenge and inspire us to live more and more in the freedom of the Glory of the children of God (Romans 8:21).

B) LOVE &FIRE

God is love. Whoever lives in love lives in God, and God in him (1 John 4:16).

Love is not just God's foremost character trait, but the essence of His whole being. God **is** love!

This means that the manifestation of His presence and His Glory can only be the manifestation of His love!

Consequently, the more we expose ourselves to the Glory of God and learn to be carriers of that Glory, the more we will experience being transformed into the image of His love.

The essence of this love is neither a special emotion nor the attracttion between two people. It is rather the devoting love of our big brother Jesus on the cross for us and for all of humanity – even for all of creation.

This is how God showed his love among us: He sent his one and only Son into the world that we might live through him. This is love: not that we loved God, but that he loved us and sent his Son as an atoning sacrifice for our sins (1 John 4:9-10).

The essence and the core of the nature of God and Jesus is the selfless "agape" love!

The more we really experience God and His Glory and are opening ourselves up for its depths, the deeper our yearning will become to give ourselves to this world – just as Jesus did. Not that we would have to go to the cross to do the work of the atonement once again – no, He has already finished that job! He died for us so that we may now live His agape-life of love on this earth.

This means that as we identify with His heart we see the world through His eyes and love as He loved.

A new command I give you: Love one another. As I have loved you, so you must love one another. By this all men will know that you are my disciples, if you love one another. (John 13:34-35)

Out of the Glory of God a consuming fire captures us. It burns away every selfish, carnal unction in us and leaves us with nothing else than passionate, devoting love.

He (Jesus) will baptize you with the Holy Spirit and with fire (Luke 3:16).

During His earthly walk, Jesus had such an impassioned love. He didn't stay unmoved by the ineffable misery of the people surrounding Him. The Bible tells us several times how He "had compassion" on them (e.g. Matthew 9:36; Luke 7:11-17 etc.). In the end He was moved to the point that He laid down His very life at an early age to obtain their, and thereby also our, redemption!

Out of God's Glory you are captured by a consuming fire of supernatural "agape" love for the people!

Having now obtained this redemption for us, it is our privilege to continue His work here on earth through the Holy Spirit:

REACHING OUT TO THE LOST

Through Jesus, God has given us a heart that seeks and saves that which is lost (Luke 19:10). This heart is to be continually kindled and activated through His spirit in us! You personally can do this repeatedly, e.g. during the time you spend with God.

We will thus love the exhausted and pined with divine passion and seek to lead them into the rest of God (Matthew 11:28[21]). We will lead the lost to salvation from hell through Jesus (John 3:16), and make them followers of Him and thus sons of God.

Again and again I realize how God is with us when we go beyond our "church walls" and search for the lost – there where they actually can be found.

That's why God confirms in wonderful and glorious ways our so-called "miracle invasions" which we as ministry hold in the streets and squares of bigger cities.

Nowadays so many people are open for the supernatural power of God. They are not afraid to be prayed for and receive healings and miracles in public!

Some of the most powerful creative miracles happened during the last couple years – and still continue to happen – when we take Jesus' great commission seriously and *go* to these people. For God so longs to show those lost people His love and if a miracle is what they need to experience His love, then He is more than willing to present them with it (*Unless you people see miraculous signs and wonders, Jesus told him, you will never believe* John 4:48).

As an example here is the report of such a "miracle invasion" held in the pedestrian area of the city of Reutlingen in 2014:

God just loves it when we make ourselves available and go – with His heart – where the sick, the lost and the bound are!

- "During the miracle invasion in the pedestrian area of Reutlingen September 20th a lot of spectacular miracles happened. People received Jesus Christ as their personal Lord and savior and some of them came to the Glory and miracle service that very night. At least 9 people got born again that day! Especially outstanding miracles were:

- A young man in a wheelchair was brought to Pastor Georg. After being asked what he wanted God to do for him, he said he would like to be more independent. For that to happen he would need to be able

---

[21] Come to me, all you who are weary and burdened, and I will give you rest.

157

to move his paralyzed left arm. After being prayed for he could move his left arm without any restrictions – something he wasn't able to do in all of his life. He himself, and all the bystanders were absolutely amazed! Thereupon, other people began to open up for the miracle-working power of God as well.

- One lady was restricted in her movement because of an implanted metal rod in her back. She was also missing an inch of bone in her right leg as a result of hip surgery. During prayer the bone grew to the same length as the one in the other leg. She is now able to walk normally without her special shoe with the heel lift.

- After also having received prayer for her back, the pain there left and the movement restrictions she had had because of the metal rod decreased remarkably.

- One man had massive problems in both his knees and needed surgery. The pain was especially excruciating in the left knee. It was as though a red-hot nail was being constantly hammered into the knee! To his great surprise, after Pastor Georg had prayed for him, the pain, as well as the associated restriction of movement, was totally gone. Even the other knee was almost totally pain and problem free!

- For an elderly man God had a word of knowledge about his problems with the lumbar region of his back. He and his wife confirmed the accuracy of this word. After being prayed for, the man walked about totally pain-free and called out, "I feel as though I'm on honeymoon! Everything feels so light and easygoing!"

- Several other people were healed and set free from pain and restrictions right there on the street. Members of the team had words of knowledge for people, who in turn gave their lives to God; legs of dissimilar length were corrected by the power of God, and people were set free from vexing spirits in their souls etc…!

God just loves it when we make ourselves available and go – with His heart – where the sick, the lost and the bound are!

CENTERS OF GOD'S GLORY

As well as for the lost, God's heart also burns for the strengthening and building up of the Body of Christ through the gifts He has put in us. John 2:17 talks about Jesus: *Zeal for your house will consume me.* God's house now is the temple of the Holy Spirit = the church = *us*!

I personally believe this fire of God that is flowing out of His Glory will establish strong centers of God's Glory all over the world during the coming years.

In these centers the sons and daughters of God who hunger for Him will gather, and at the same time multitudes of unsaved people will be drawn to them.

About three years ago I saw several of such centers ("pockets") of Glory in a powerful inner vision. From out of them, spiritual "governmental authority" will literally be executed over whole territories and nations. Mighty signs and wonders happen in and through them, people get saved, and whole regions and nations will be influenced to live according to the requirements of God's kingdom.

Churches which have decided to constantly host the Glory of God in their midst will become spiritual "government centers" for whole regions and nations.

It is God's plan for these end times to establish and keep up such centers from where the knowledge of the Glory of the Lord radiates until it finally covers the whole earth. As these centers unite with each other and flow together, even all the "gaps" in between them will be totally flooded with the Glory of God.

At the same time, I saw the need for those who are called to dwell continually in such a center of the Glory, to stay focused on the "Rose", i.e. Jesus (Song of Solomon 2:1) – and drink in His sweet fragrance. This way they will be able to keep themselves on the highest possible spiritual level, constantly obtaining new strength, peace, freedom and stability.

Through the fragrance of this Rose we climb up time and again to the heavenly realms of Glory to reign from there!

These Glory centers will not just be pastorally led churches or ministries but apostolically-prophetically led "government centers"[22].

The apostolic and prophetic ministries will be the foundation of the "Glory centers" of the end times!

They will be grounded and nourished by the fullness of the fivefold ministry (apostles, prophets, evangelists, pastors and teachers – Ephesians 4:11-16), as well as by the whole range of the spiritual gifts (see as an example 1 Corinthians 12), whereby the foundation is the apostolic and the prophetic ministry (Ephesians 2:20; Zechariah 4). The main goal of all these ministry gifts is to lead the church of Jesus into a deeper revelation of and to a deeper love for our Lord Himself – until the full likeness of Christ is gained in all of us (Galatians 4:19).

In addition, new spiritual songs of praise, proclamations, worship and Glory will emerge from these centers because every new move of the Spirit initiated in heaven always brings forth a new heavenly sound which helps bring God's new movement out of the spiritual realm down to us here on earth.

A new sound in our praise and worship will come forth out of the Glory!

In these centers, it will not be first and foremost about getting as many people together as possible (even though God of course wants as many as possible in the boat!). It will rather be about gathering as many spiritually hungry, devoted, fiery sons and daughters of God together who are ready to surrender totally to the consuming fire of God's love, i.e. Jesus Himself, and His Glory. These will have no other goal for their lives other than to bring the Glory of God down to earth right there where God has placed them!

---

[22]In chapter 12 (Stuttgart 21) I gave testimony about this governmental authority being at work.

This end-time army will care more about true spiritual breakthroughs rather than about visible success in the natural. And they will be determined to execute their authority in Christ from out of the spirit realm over all the realms of the natural.

In this season those who hunger for God and for nothing else are being called together!

Through these Glory Centers, spirits and mental edifices over whole nations will be brought down, and ungodly "strongholds" will be replaced by the spirit of love and faith as well as godly thinking and values – even if not every single citizen of a nation will turn to Christ.

Let's realize: Crucial changes in a nation emerge from the spiritual realm, not from the natural realm, e.g. in the political arena. This doesn't mean to say that Christians cannot be called to be active in all areas of society – quite the contrary! However, the key to power is found in the throne room of God, which is the true "Power and Glory Center" of the whole universe!

Now is the time that God is calling for a company of forerunners and pioneers of this ever increasing and rising Glory! They will be activated from out of the Glory realm to start apostolic-prophetic Glory centers everywhere on the planet.

When I asked God about 6 years ago what my ministry would look like in the future, He answered me: You will help to build and inspire a movement which consists of people who are hungry for the Glory of God, and who reach out in a childlike spirit to all the supernatural that is contained therein! God will call whole churches into this movement and these churches will see their highest goal in permanently housing the Glory of God!

THE COVENANT LOVE OF GOD

All these spiritually hungry, more and more emerging sons of God will be united by the invisible tie of Jesus' self-abandoning agape-love.

God spoke to me early in 2014: *The covenant-love of the Father unites and brings growth!* This means that just as God has made a covenant with us through Jesus, so are we in covenant with one another and with His Body!

This covenant is not about soulish bondages, control or even manipulation. In fact, Jesus' love causes an ever deeper fusing of the children of God with one another which comes out of staying focused on their Lord and having a consciousness of a shared mission.

The covenant-love of God ties together the hungry sons and daughters in unity; and thus causes growth in all areas!

You can't be in covenant with Jesus (the head of the Body) long-term without at the same time being in covenant with His Body, and vice versa.

Jesus and His Body are inseparably linked to each other. What would a headless body or a bodiless head be? They would be nonviable = dead!

This means your covenant relationship with Jesus deepens all the more when your covenant relationship with His Body here on earth deepens. In this respect, we are continually growing under the influence of His glory.

Unreserved faith in the love of God (1 Corinthians 13:7) produces unreserved devotion!

Furthermore, I don't believe that this coming move will only consist out of one single ministry or be led by only one anointed vessel. I believe rather that many apostolic-prophetic Glory bearers will arise worldwide and will build up and lead such Glory centers or whole networks of Glory centers, wherever God has placed them.

The more these Glory bearers are linked and spiritually connected to each other, the more powerful the global network of Glory will become. God is now starting to span it around the globe – so that very soon the whole earth will be filled with the knowledge of the Glory of the Lord as the waters cover the sea!

Entire nations are being called into following the Glory of God (Matthew 28:19; Mark 16:15). As I said before, this doesn't necessarily mean that every single person of a nation will be saved. However, whole nations will consciously or unconsciously follow the pillar of cloud and fire of the Glory of God! This will be just because in their midst there are centers with sons of God releasing His Glory with power into these nations and thus establishing it in the spiritual "airspace".

In the process, the physical nation of God's chosen people – Israel, the trunk out of which we heathen Christians have come out of – will play a vital and increasing role in the end times (see Romans 11; Romans 15:27 etc.). The space is missing in this book for me though to explain these things in more detail.

Let the fire of God's heart again and again ignite you for His church, the lost as well as the nations! It's in you!

Summing up, we can say from out of the Glory there comes a fire of cleansing and a fire of compassion, which works in us a continuing, everlasting burning for the things that are on God's heart – namely His Church, the lost and the nations of this world.

Matthew 6:33 says that if we seek first His kingdom (i.e. the things which are on His heart), everything else we need in the natural and for ourselves will be added to us!

Therefore, never stop reaching out intensely for this fire of God which longs to burn ever stronger in your heart and in the midst of Jesus' church: Luke 12:49 *I have come to bring fire on the earth, and how I wish it were already kindled!*

C) POWER

Heaven is a place of endless power and energy. Just meditate on the revelation of the throne room in Revelation 4! There it speaks of flashes of lightning and thunder that emerge from the throne of God. You will agree with me, that there is hardly anything of greater energy than a flash of lightning!

This means, in other words, that heaven is continually under energetic high-voltage, and enormous impulses of energy are constantly discharging from the throne of God with tremendous thunder.

Once I saw such flashes of lightning in a vision emerging from God's throne. God explained to me that each of these flashes would contain the energy for a certain initiative, a certain miracle or a certain project here on earth. Whosoever would "catch" such a flash, would receive with it the *power and capability* to execute this heavenly impulse here on earth. So, let's catch "flashes"!

Undoubtedly it is an utter illusion to believe that you can come closer to God without inevitably getting into contact with an endless "force field"!

Heaven is saturated with a power loaded atmosphere – what about our services?

Little neat church services in a totally harmless, weak atmosphere are for sure not services where God's Glory truly manifests!

However, don't get me wrong, this chapter explains that God's Glory manifests in various ways – including the delicate and even tender aspects of the love of the Father. Nevertheless, God's power certainly is an essential "ingredient" of the tangible Glory and presence of God and it permeates every other aspect.

When we reach out for the Glory of God in our lives and in our churches we shouldn't be surprised if mighty releases and discharges of the power of God occur with it. These could easily overwhelm our physical bodies and can thus be followed by such manifestations as the coming out of demons, jerking, trembling or falling.

Sometimes, for example, people ask, "Why do some people in your services fall over?" My simple answer to this is, "Because they are not able to keep standing!" I do not know of a more precise answer, because that is exactly what happens – the natural body collapses under the discharging flashes of God's Glory.

However the discharge of power *into* us is not all there is to it. In fact we ourselves, through receiving God's power, become carriers of this power. As a natural consequence we will experience that this power discharges through and *out of us* wherever it is needed, and whenever we put it to action – e.g. by the laying on of hands or speaking out in authority!

This actually is the very "natural" life of a disciple of Jesus – to be continually "recharged" with the power of God and then passing it on to others! It was the same with Jesus when He walked the earth. He frequently got "charged" with power during His personal time with the Father and then He went to the people and the power "discharged" from Him. See, for example, Luke 6:19 *and the people all tried to touch him, because power was coming from him and healing them all.* See also Mark 5:30; Luke 4:14; Luke 4:36; Luke 5:17; Luke 9:1 etc.!

A Christ-like life is mainly about getting "charged" over and over again with the power of God and then passing the power on to our surroundings in different forms!

In order for "Christianity" to be born at all, the first disciples had to first "receive power" (Acts 1:8) – without that power they could do nothing, so they had to stay in Jerusalem until they had received it.

Since the completion of Jesus' atonement – that is since His ascension and the descending of His Holy Spirit to earth – we as sons and daughters of God have constant unlimited access to any power that is in God (see Hebrews 10:19), meaning having access to Himself, who is the power center of the entire universe!

It is surely not God's plan for us to just receive a thrust of power every once in a while in some revival. The power of God is our essential daily bread of life! We may and should in faith "take it by force" over and over again (Matthew 11:12) – during our private time with God as well as in our church services!

Strictly speaking there is no "Christianity" without power. *Christ* – the title of our savior – means "The One anointed with power" which means that a Jesus *Christ* without power is non-existent!

As Christians we believe in *Jesus Christ* – not only in *Jesus* and not only in any "*Christ*", but in *Jesus Christ*!

God once showed me how the devil has been working for 2000 years with all his tricks to separate "Jesus" from "Christ". On the one hand he infiltrates Christians with the picture of a sweet, harmless, religious, powerless Jesus or a Jesus Christ who actually has power but is so far above us in heaven that there is no real connection to us.

He makes Christians afraid of God's power, and teaches them to protect themselves through all kinds of theologies, programs and rituals. This way they can no longer become too dangerous for the devil and his demons.

On the other hand the devil tries to offer a "Christ" detached from Jesus – but endowed with certain power. This "Christ" however is not our redeemer and thus not our legitimate divine source of power (see Matthew 24:5 and Matthew 24:24). That's what frequently happens in new age groups or pseudo-Christian cults.

What is very important for us as Christians is that we do not get ensnared by the first deception out of fear of the second one!

In God's eyes, a powerless "Christianity", i.e. a church presenting and theologically justifying a powerless "Jesus", is as equally wrong as an obviously false Christ. Behind both deceptions the spirit of antichrist is at work, a spirit that will not confess "*Jesus Christ*" as meaning "Jesus, the One anointed with power" *who has come in the flesh* (1 John 4:2)!

Even if it challenges us, we have to decide: Do we want the Jesus Christ in our midst that is being revealed to us throughout the Bible? Do we want His Glory with all that goes with it? If so, then let us be ready to experience the power of God in our midst, to be changed and to be charged by it as never before in order to effectively get this world in touch with heaven!

We will then discover that this is the most rewarding and best thing we can imagine for our life here on this earth!

D) EXCELLENCE & DIGNITY

"Splendor and majesty are before him; strength and joy in his dwelling place..." (1 Chronicles 16:27)

If your heart is open, receptive and ready to learn, it won't take long for the character traits of the person you are hanging out with to "rub off" on you!

If you are continuously hanging out with God in His Glory, His Being shining on you then certainly every area of your life and being will get permeated more and more by His life and Being. Of course this means also that more and more of His excellence and dignity will reflect from you – for He is not a poor, ugly, blemished God, but the personified beauty, perfection and fullness!

His presence will thus change your entire life into the same excellence, beauty, fullness and perfection.

The more you "hang out with God", the more you will reflect His character of excellence and dignity!

Your entire character will be formed by His. This means you will no longer be satisfied with mediocre, unclean stuff or with a dissolute, messy and undisciplined life. On the contrary, you will be exceedingly eager to reflect at every single moment His character in all facets of your life!

Of course this renewal is a process, but it is unstoppable in those who expose themselves continually to God's Glory.

As already mentioned this is not about an outward behavior therapy, although, of course, the Holy Spirit might show you specific patterns in your life that have to consciously be corrected. Most changes are rather derived from the ever increasing intimate fellowship with His Person and radiance (=Glory) in the Spirit!

The Spirit of God and His Glory is upon you and within you as His son/daughter, and He will lead you and guide your life step-by-step on the paths of excellence whilst also eliminating all kinds of destructive thinking and behavior. It is so easy if you just keep your eyes on Him!

DIGNITY

The more you become aware of your *dignity* as a son/daughter of God, the less you will be willing to accept things in your life which really are "beneath your dignity" – such as addictions, compulsions, fears, lack of discipline, licentiousness etc.

To become aware of your "dignity" doesn't mean to become haughty[23], but rather to realize more and more whom you represent here on this earth and what incredible calling comes with that. You are a representative of the King of Kings, the Lord of Glory, and your destiny as His son is to spread His mighty and glorious kingdom in this world, presenting God Himself!

T.L. Osborn puts it very well: "Before you were born, you existed in His thoughts and His plan. He knew the world would need you now, at this time and hour. He planned you for a special purpose nobody else could fulfill here on earth. No one can do what you are supposed to do here on earth."[24]

Let that melt in your mouth!

The more you become aware of this dignity, the more your life will turn towards divine excellence, and the less you will fall for the efforts of the deceiver to pull you into an inferior life of mediocrity, bondage or even sin.

Knowing who God is and knowing who we are, are the two sides of the same coin!

You will actually experience more and more success in all you put your hands to because *the Spirit of glory and of God rests upon you* (1 Peter 4:14) – which is the Spirit of His favor, the spirit of sonship. You are a person of kingly dignity (see Revelations 1:6)!

In the Glory you realize more and more who God is. Since God is now living in you through Jesus and the Holy Spirit, you automatically increasingly realize who you *yourself* are in God's plan and accordingly who you have truly *always been!*

The true "you" as a spiritual personality is evolving more and more – you who has already been "known" by God before you were formed in your mother's womb – (Psalms 139:13-16; Jeremiah 1:5)!

Without knowing God this is impossible because your identity is rooted in God. At the same time it is impossible to really know God and thereby not

---

[23]See Chapter 25 "A Word of Wisdom".
[24]T.L.Osborn "You are God's Best"

know yourself because God, through Jesus Christ, has connected Himself inseparably to us.

Knowing who God is and knowing who we are in Christ are the two sides of the same precious coin!

21

SIGNS AND WONDERS

The whole topic of signs and wonders in Christendom still doesn't have the significance it should actually have according to the Word of God.

We should by no means underestimate the importance of signs and wonders!

It is absolutely correct, as often emphasized, that the evolvement and growth of the fruits of the spirit (like love, joy, peace, patience, kindness, goodness, faithfulness, gentleness and self-control – Galatians 5:22) are vital indicators of our progress in our walk with Christ. If a person truly is born-again, the Holy Spirit within his spirit will always prompt this transformation from the inside out. This means that Christ in us wants to be revealed more and more through us with His perfect personality, i.e. with all His divine character traits!

The works of the flesh listed in Galatians 5:19 onwards[25] do not reflect Him, so His Spirit will therefore increasingly eliminate them from our lives, eventually taking us over from the inside.

If that doesn't happen, even the greatest miracles that happen through us will be of little effect because our still dominant natural personality will partly overshadow the revelation of the person of God in the eyes of the people

---

[25] *The acts of the sinful nature are obvious: sexual immorality, impurity and debauchery; idolatry and witchcraft; hatred, discord, jealousy, fits of rage, selfish ambition, dissensions, factions and envy; drunkenness, orgies, and the like.*

around us, and lasting fruit can only come forth in a reduced measure. Jesus, however, wants us to bear much lasting fruit (John 15:8+16).

So, if we cultivate a one-sided zeal for supernatural signs and wonders, we will not fulfill God's full plan for our life. We need the same keenness for the fruit of the Spirit as well as for the spiritual gifts and acts of power. 1 Corinthians 14:1 talks about this combination: *Follow the way of love and eagerly desire spiritual gifts.*

Signs and wonders alone, by the way, are also no clear evidence that the Glory of God manifests in fullness. As mentioned before, a healing or a miracle can also be ministered through a specific spiritual gift (see 1 Corinthians 12:9-11).

Furthermore, miracles can happen solely through the preaching of the Word if it is combined with faith in the heart of the listener.

All this is possible without us truly having to live in the realm of Glory, and without the Glory noticeably manifesting in our meetings.

It is utterly impossible for the Glory of God to truly manifest in a meeting or in a situation without signs and wonders happening in one way or the other.

On the other hand, it is completely impossible that the Glory of God really manifests around a person or in a meeting without supernatural things like signs and wonders happening in one way or other. They happen in the Glory even when there is no special gift active, or when the faith level based on the Word in a congregation is low.

Fact is, that we serve a God who is supernatural through and through and when His immediate presence manifests, supernatural occurrences automatically follow.

Therefore, making light of the significance of and the desire for signs and wonders in the church of Jesus Christ, equals hindering the Glory from gaining space in fullness within our churches.

If people or churches say, "We also have the Glory of God in our midst – but we don't need signs and wonders to come with it", then you know that this statement is made in total ignorance of what the Glory of God (and who God Himself) truly is. [26]

The reason for the Bible being loaded with accounts of all kinds of signs and wonders is to spark our appetite and make us hungry for even more power and supernatural substance in our lives, churches and ministries.

And, right now, this is exactly what God is increasingly setting in motion in us, His Body...

Another thing – the moment we have made the decision for signs and wonders, we step out onto the water like Peter. We come out of the vague general state of our faith into the realm of verifiability (even for outsiders). In other words, we expose ourselves to a certain faith- risk that maybe "it could not work", because, of course, there is no way we can produce any signs and miracles in our own power!

For example, if we, in faith, announce healing meetings and nobody gets healed then this could really get embarrassing – at least those who seek healing won't continue to come for long...

This is the reason why many Christians and spiritual leaders shy away from making signs and wonders a crucial part of their lives and ministries. I too gave into the lies of the devil for years, believing that this life on the water would be way too challenging and loaded with attacks – and therefore not for me.

The truth however is that exactly our positioning "on the water" causes the strongest supernatural things to happen – that "what no eye has seen, what no ear has heard and what has not come into a human's heart"!

God will never forsake us if we take a risk for His sake. No, in fact He is longing for us to finally step out of our boat of human security.

---

[26] At this point I don't want to go deeper into the theological doctrine saying that signs and wonders have ceased with the first generation of Christians and with the completion of the Bible (so called cessationism). Just let me mention, the Bible itself doesn't give the slightest hint for this. On the contrary, Jesus encourages us to fulfill our calling in faithful expectancy of signs and wonders until He returns (Mark 16:15-20). A cessationist will, however, mostly always see his doctrine confirmed in his life which means he will probably never experience any signs or miracles...

The fear of "nothing happening" is completely unfounded when we are resolutely fulfilling our God-given mission. In fact, God rejoices over every step of faith we take and He is more than willing to open the floodgates of heaven through us into this world.

The moment we decide for a lifestyle of miracles we put ourselves at risk – and it is exactly this tension that is needed to "bring heaven down" into our lives.

Generally speaking, faith that doesn't take a risk is of little substance. If we do not expect any measurable effects from our faith and don't aim for results, then our "faith" will ultimately remain undeveloped. We will be left weak and frustrated if we don't dare to time and again, walk on water to prove its carrying capacity and, in fact, I don't know of any better proof than the broad spectrum of supernatural signs and wonders!

Yes, the moment we make signs, wonders and miracles our lifestyle, we'll live under a permanent "reality-check". This, however, in turn, lets our life become a real fulfilling and exciting faith-adventure!

Ideally, the spiritual leaders in the churches should be the ones to start walking in this direction as only they can create a lasting atmosphere where God's supernatural activities are welcomed and desired.

Individual Christians can of course make headway in this, but as long as their spiritual leader will not open up and reach out for this realm, it will be difficult for them who yearn for more to come forth in this.

However, I believe that now is the time when more and more spiritual leaders and entire churches are stretching out toward the supernatural. They are making the decision to see the manifestation of signs and wonders on a regular basis in their congregations and fellowships.

To summarize, we can say that the manifestation of God's Glory is closely connected to signs, wonders and miracles. While you might see signs and wonders manifest without the Glory, it is utterly impossible that the Glory manifests without signs, wonders and miracles happening.

Oftentimes, seizing signs and wonders by faith will increase the manifestation of God's Glory in a meeting. Sometimes it will even initiate it (the Glory's manifestation) –mainly in meetings where the people are not yet used to the presence of God, especially in evangelistic settings.

You cannot separate the Glory of God from the manifestation of signs and wonders.

Furthermore, according to my experience, certain kinds of signs and wonders will only ever be seen when the Glory of God manifests.

The primary focus of our hunger therefore shouldn't be the signs and wonders as such and as an end in itself, but God Himself, His presence and manifest Glory in our lives and in our congregations. And with that comes His love for the people whom He so desperately wants to be saved, healed and delivered.

As a preacher once put it: Going after God's love for the people more than pursuing to have power in your own hands, releases the anointing for miracles.

However, once we have touched the realm of His manifest presence and Glory, abundant signs and wonders will automatically follow: *He performs wonders that cannot be fathomed, miracles that cannot be counted* (Job 5:9).

It will then be absolutely natural for the sake of the sick, bound and unsaved people to pursue an ever increasing manifestation of these miracles…

In closing, here is an illustration: If someone enters a high voltage power field he won't be able to avoid being hit by one or the other discharge of power from the force field. Signs and wonders are like the discharge from the energy power field which surrounds the center of God's Glory.

They are spiritual high energy flashes of lightning constantly emanating from the throne of God. So, when you bring the Glory of God's throne (spiritually speaking) into a life or a meeting then the flashes won't be far off. Immerse a son of God into the power field of the throne room (see Revelations 4), and miracles are bound to happen.

Then more miracles are followed by more hunger, and with greater hunger comes greater Glory and, consequently, more miracles, and more hunger…and so on. This is a continual upward spiral in which the church of Jesus Christ will operate in the end times as the army of the sons of God is being revealed.

This is exactly what we are experiencing since 2010.

Although I have conducted healing services regularly since 2006 and seen people getting healed and saved, in 2010 God led me (as already mentioned in the first part of this book) into a deeper pursuit of His supernatural workings in my life and ministry. I just knew deep inside there must be something more. I therefore increasingly exposed myself to services and messages where a stronger supernatural substance was more tangible than the one I had already experienced myself.

A prophet once said about the prophetic, "The prophetic is rather caught than taught". Exactly the same is true for the whole realm of signs and wonders, as well as for any other realm of the Glory of God.

One of God's favorite ways to lead you into a new dimension is to position you around someone who already lives deeper in this realm than you do (let's call it the Elisha-principle).

This is exactly what He did with me.

Anyhow, I can honestly tell you that there is absolutely nothing that qualifies me more to experience His signs and miracles than any other son or daughter of God. Nothing can, in any way, keep you from experiencing the same – and even greater things than you see in me or others.

OUTPOURING OF MIRACLES

After an intense time of reaching out, very suddenly God opened a completely new field of power around me. You could also call it a totally new realm of glory.

The visible signs were obvious. Increased numbers of healings and miracles were occurring at shorter intervals than ever before. Many things that were happening we had never seen before, e.g. one young woman's finger grew out to full length. It had been underdeveloped and only half as long as the others due to an operation on the tendon in her childhood. Within one second it "grew out" to its correct length, size and form.

An eye which was lopsided and drooping due to an accident became normal after the laying on of hands. Cancers and tumors vanished; a leg which had been lame due to a severed nerve was restored with full movement; a deaf ear due to a severed auditory nerve was able to hear again. After prayer a woman who was paralyzed on one side after a stroke was healed and she ran around and around the room. Another woman was healed from Erb's palsy (shoulder-arm-paralysis due to a birth defect). A young man who was in a coma as a result of a severe accident and had a very low chance of survival was completely restored within a short period of time after prayer over the phone. A "myriad" of bones came back into God's order through creative miracles. Numerous medically incurable diseases and problems were healed "just like that".[27]

It is also noteworthy that these miracles did not happen only through me as a special healing minister but through numerous members of our church. Full of enthusiasm, some of them took the power and Glory of God directly to their work places and even to the streets and squares in the region where they experienced many truly spectacular things. This shows us that in this "era of Glory" God does not only want to perform signs and wonders through a few "specialists" but through every single one of His children. None of us is either inept or better qualified. The only reason God installed the fivefold ministry in a special way (Ephesians 4:11) was for training and equipment. We all live in the same "glory cloud" when we connect in faith with this reality and with each other.

Once you have experienced a breakthrough of the Glory of God in your life you are hungry for more!

Exactly this "cloud" manifests in this outpouring in an extremely thick manner. I quickly realized that we were dealing with a completely new dimension of the Glory of God that was now manifesting in our services.

---

[27]The list could be continued endlessly but you can read up on some of the most powerful incidents in our "Miracle News Reports" at www.glorylife.de which we started at that time. As a matter of fact these types of miracles have increased big time in number and variety since the outpouring first started.

177

I knew this is the substance I was longing for, and this substance would change everything around us.

Once you have experienced such a breakthrough you hunger for more.

So, I knew that we had to continue on this path. I would never again let go of the Glory of God but seize it no matter the cost, allowing the Holy Spirit to continuously take me to new dimensions…

A few reports follow, written down personally by those who had been healed during the initial period of the outpouring:

Cancer completely gone

I suffered from cancer in the lymph nodes under my armpit as well as in my jaw. I was treated with radiation and chemotherapy. After the pastor had prayed for me on Sunday the doctor could not find any more malignant cells in my body.

On top of that, a chronic wound on the back of my head that had not closed up for a long time was completely healed, and very severe neuralgia in my head and body is completely gone. Thank you, Jesus! G.

Spontaneous muscle regeneration

Due to an injury, the muscles in my upper arm were completely degenerated – just skin and bone. I could not even lift my arm properly. However, in the miracle service I experienced how muscle mass grew supernaturally, and at the end of the service I was able to lift up my arm again and also had a visible biceps. G.S.

God's creative power: Birth defect completely gone

I was born just as the doctor was having his lunch break. My mom heard him say, "Does she need to have the baby now?" Because he was in such a hurry he delivered me with forceps, forcibly pulling on my arm. Two weeks later my father noticed that I did not move that arm and my parents took me to the pediatrician. It was too late, the arm had already turned blue and looked defunct.

They immediately put my arm in a cast for three years but it did not help. I was able to move the hand on that arm and through special physiotherapy was able to improve dexterity. However, I was never able to really lift that arm, it was lame (so-called Erb's palsy, caused by an irreparable injury of nerve cords at birth).

After I had been prayed for at the healing service, I was immediately able to lift up my arm all the way. It is a divine miracle because my formerly useless arm now functions perfectly. I am so happy and thankful. Now I am able to take things off the top shelf without anybody's help. For all these decades I had not been able to do that. B.P.

Do not need glasses any more

Since I go to the church, the Holy Spirit again and again works in certain places of my body that are out of order. After one healing service the anointing started to massage my eyes. Over a few months this increased and the shortsightedness in both of my eyes (approx. 3 diopters) receded. Also, a starting presbyopia vanished. In the meantime, I have thrown away my glasses. It is such a marvelous gift to be able to see so clearly, to see the overhead transparencies in church as well as any fine print directly in front of me. A.K.

Lump vanished spontaneously

I had a lump under my breast, about 1 ½ inches, which had been diagnosed by the doctor. After laying on of hands in Jesus Name, I could not feel the lump any more – it was completely gone. In the meantime I have also received a written confirmation from my doctor that there is no more evidence of that lump. I.L.

Healed from hemiplegia

I fell unconscious in the bathroom. When I woke up my right side was paralyzed (stroke). I was taken to the ICU in hospital. The doctors said, due to my extremely high blood pressure I actually should not have survived... Of course, that Sunday I was not able to go to the (healing) service but God allowed me to be part of it through an open vision. That really strengthened me. When I was released from hospital a few days later, I was handicapped in many ways due to my paralysis. On Thursday, 17 April, I dragged myself to church anyway because I suddenly had a strong impulse to go. At the end,I let the pastor and his wife pray for me. Suddenly I felt a strong heat go through my right side. I slowly started moving and it worked, I walked a few steps holding the pastor's hand – then he let go of my hand and finally I ran through the whole room, jumping and dancing joyfully. It was awesome. Since then I can move normally again and do everything, even ironing and driving my car. The next day I went to the doctor. When he read the report that the doctors in hospital had written, he said that they must have "grossly exaggerated" in the diagnosis. "Forget this report", the doctor said after I had explained to him that I had been healed supernaturally. He even did not consider the scheduled rehab to be necessary any more. Thank you, Jesus who works miracles. L.S.

Healed from poor eyesight

While I was going to university my eyesight grew steadily worse. I went to the ophthalmologist who had prescribed new glasses for me just the year before. He was quite concerned as my eyesight had declined by 2.5 diopters to -4. I needed new glasses again.

During the Sunday morning service Pastor Georg had the impression that he needed to pray for eyes. I went forward. When he put his hand on my eyes and prayed for me I felt heat all over my body. I did not know what happened.

In the days that followed I noticed that I could see much better again. I took my glasses off. From then on I was able to continue and finish my studies without them. I can now see clearly without glasses.

When I went back home to the Republic of Georgia my doctor thought that I had had a "secret" operation in Germany. He could not believe what God had done for me. M.K.

That is just a small selection of miracle reports from people who had been healed in the first few months after the beginning of the outpouring of miracles. They wrote them down personally and sent them to us. All honor belongs to our wonderful Lord Jesus Christ.

EXODUS FROM "EGYPT"" – SIGNS AND WONDERS

Let me show you another important role of signs and wonders in the plan of God.

From a spiritual point of view, Israel's exodus out of Egypt and the taking of Canaan, their Promised Land, is a prophetic Old Testament foreshadow of our New Covenant lives in Jesus. The Holy Spirit also leads *us* out of *our* "Egypt", namely sin, the enslavement under the powers of darkness, worldliness, natural emotions and soulish life, religion etc. (see Ephesians 2:1-5; Colossians 1:13-14).

This takes place in our spirit in the blink of an eye when we are born again and keeps on developing and growing for the rest of our lives in our souls and our outward man.

This means that every Christian who truly is a follower of Jesus is on a continual journey out of his "Egypt" as far as his soul and body is concerned. And, according to the Bible, it is God's plan that signs and wonders follow us on this journey in the same way as they followed Moses:

"When you (Moses) return…see that you perform before Pharaoh all the wonders I have given you the power to do." (Exodus 4:21)

As with Moses, God has given us the power to do signs and wonders that are to accompany us on our gradual exodus from our (spiritual) Egypt.

In New Covenant language this means to confront the powers of darkness that are trying to keep the sons and daughters of God in enslavement and darkness *with signs and wonders.* The devil then has no choice but to let them go into their freedom.

As with Moses, God has given us an array of different kinds of miracles into our hands (read more in the following section). So now we have the privilege to use these gifts to emphasize the call of the Father *"into the freedom and glory of the children of God"* (Romans 8:21) and to give it a voice in people's hearts. and also in the unseen world.

It simply needs spiritual power to bring people out of their personal "Egypt". This power expresses itself, amongst other things, in verifiable signs, wonders and mighty deeds.

In Deuteronomy 7:19 God speaks in retrospect to the people of Israel through Moses, saying: *You saw with your own eyes the great trials, the signs and wonders, the mighty hand and outstretched arm, with which the Lord your God brought you out.*

Looking back on our journey with God, signs and wonders are like "mementoes" through which He intends to permanently remind us of His endless mercy and grace. They also continuously encourage us for the journey still ahead. Let us thus stretch out full of anticipation and joy, expecting to accumulate as many supernatural mementoes on our journey as possible.

TAKING OVER THE PROMISED LAND: SIGNS AND WONDERS

Secondly, the leading of the Holy Spirit is not only ***Out*** *of Egypt!* –but also, at the same time, ***Into*** *the Promised Land!*

Actually, there should have been only a few weeks between Israel's exodus from Egypt and the entry into the Promised Land. However, Israel's unbelief prolonged this period to 40 years. It should not be like that with us as children of the New Covenant. In Christ, both the exodus out of the old and the entering into the new, or rather the taking of the Promised Land, happens simultaneously.

We must not only leave the old behind but also take over our new promised land. This refers to the expression of "the Kingdom of God" which is to become reality here on earth through us (and only through us). *I will give you every place where you set your foot, as I promised Moses.* Joshua 1:3

God has a specific plan for your life, a customized task which only you and no one else can fulfill. To align yourself with this plan and to fulfill this task means taking your promised land.

This take-over of land should also be accompanied by signs and wonders, according to the plan of God. That is why Joshua says to the people just prior to their crossing the river Jordan into the Promised Land, *"Consecrate yourselves, for tomorrow the Lord will do amazing things among you."* (Joshua 3:5). And as you will read in the following chapters of the book of Joshua that is exactly what God ended up doing in abundance.

Signs and wonders frighten the "giants" in your promised land and cause them to flee.

During the *exodus* out of Egypt, the purpose of miracles was to get Pharaoh (= devil) to let the people go. In the same way, for the *take-over* of the land, the purpose of miracles is to first intimidate the "giants" (= demonic powers) in our promised land and then to drive them out.

Looking at Ephesians 3:10, we could also say that signs and wonders are a part of the Full Gospel and have been given to the Body of Christ today to, in every respect, *make known the manifold wisdom of God to the rulers and authorities in the heavenly realms.* They play an essential role in enforcing the victory Jesus has already won on the Cross for humanity.

"Flanked" by signs and wonders, the end-time church, the army of the sons and daughters of God (Joel 2:5-11) will unstoppably leave behind any characteristics and influences of the powers of darkness and, at the same time, demonstrate and spread the Kingdom of God in power on this earth – as in heaven so on earth.

NEW "ROOMS" OF MIRACLES

My Father's house has many rooms; if that were not so, would I have told you that I am going there to prepare a place for you? And if I go and prepare a place for you, I will come back and take you to be with me that you also may be where I am. You know the way to the place where I am going (John 14:2-5).

Jesus is making some astonishing statements here. On the one hand, He describes the "house of the Father", which is the dwelling place of God; i.e. heaven. He goes on to say that in this "house" there are many mansions or rooms (depending on the translation). In other words, in the part of the spiritual world which we call "heaven" there is not just only one room (e.g. the throne room of God) but many rooms.

Then Jesus says that He will, through His death, resurrection and ascension to heaven go before to prepare a dwelling place for us, His disciples. You could even say, to equip us with a "residence permit" for all rooms that are there.

This residence permit is valid for anyone who believes in His finished redemptive work. Jesus has purchased it for us by sprinkling His Blood once and for all as an effective sacrifice on the heavenly altar in the Holy of Holies (see Hebrews 9:12).

After having worked out our salvation, Jesus now continues to say in John 14, He will *come again to take us with him* to where He already is, since His ascension.

This statement can certainly *also* be used to refer to the bodily return of Jesus, but in the context of John 14, this is definitely not the only meaning.

The whole chapter talks about the sending of the Holy Spirit, the advocate and "representative" of Jesus to come into us so that through Him Jesus Himself is living within us (John 14:16-20;23;28). When Jesus says in John 14 that He will "come to us" again, He is here talking about coming to us *in the person of the Holy Spirit*.

This then means that the whole prophecy of Jesus in regard to "God's rooms" has been *fulfilled at Pentecost*.

Ten days after His ascension Jesus returned, namely in the form of the Holy Spirit – into the spirits of the disciples who were born again at that moment through that very Spirit.[28]

Jesus then prophecies in John 14:3 that He will *take us to be with Him that we also may be where He is.* This can only mean that in God's descent in the Holy Spirit an ascent simultaneously takes place of those who receive this Holy Spirit. This ascent is into heaven, namely into God Himself, the house of the Father with the many rooms (remember also what has been said in Part II, Chapter 11).

The Holy Spirit comes down as a substitute for Jesus and takes us up (in the spirit) to heavenly places – exactly to the place where Jesus is now (see Ephesians 2:6). You are already there right at this moment! Why don't you start "looking around" a bit…?

The end of Jesus' high priestly prayer in John 17:24 is very fitting in this context. It says, *Father, I want those you have given me to be with me **where I am**, and to **see my glory**, the glory you have given me…*

The way to these heavenly rooms is Jesus Himself. When Thomas objects, saying, *Lord we don't know where you are going, so how can we know the way?*, He makes this very clear (John 14:4-6).

In heaven there are an infinite number of spiritual "rooms".
Through Jesus you now may freely enter all of them.

Jesus is the one and only way to the Father (verse 6) and through Him, in the Holy Spirit, we may enter all rooms freely that are in our Father's house in heaven.

---

[28] I do not believe that there was even one disciple who had been "born again" in a true sense before Pentecost happened. Since the completion of Jesus' redemptive work was the prerequisite for salvation, it became effective only with the sending of the Holy Spirit – which is the living person of Jesus Christ in spiritual form – into the hearts of the disciples. However, this does not mean that there would not also be additional "infillings" of the Holy Spirit that are separate from the new birth (e.g. Acts 4:31). Paul even encourages us as born-again Christians to be filled afresh with the Holy Spirit again and again (Ephesians 5:18). But at the hour of birth of the church the new birth and the infilling with the Holy Spirit coincided as one glorious happening.

Now, when we enter these spiritual rooms, we immerse ourselves in a certain spiritual substance that corresponds exactly with that room we are entering. In the room of healing we are immersing ourselves in the substance of healing, in the room of joy in the substance of heavenly joy etc...

So, when we then act on this earth from out of our staying in a certain spiritual room, it will be exactly this room's specific spiritual substance that will be released. You could also say, *we are clothed with a very specific substance and power while we are staying in a certain spiritual room in the Father's house.*

According to Jesus' words we can just enter any of these rooms through faith in His accomplished work. We take a hold of it and become aware of it through the communion of our spirit with the Holy Spirit – and "boom", we are there. God has really made it incredibly easy for us...

I believe that in heaven, meaning in the Glory of God, there is an infinite number of rooms.

For example, there are rooms containing nothing but pure joy, fullness and ease. If you enter into these rooms you are filled with supernatural joy to overflowing (see 1 Chronicles 16:27; Acts 2:28).

There are rooms where you will be overwhelmed with love and compassion for people (see 2 Corinthians 5:14) as Jesus was in Matthew 9:36. This will cause people around you to be touched and changed by this special love that is flowing through you from that moment on.

There are heavenly rooms of intimacy with God, or rooms where we receive great authority to reign with Christ in this life (Romans 5:17; Job 22:28). We are filled with the appropriate effectiveness in the rooms of intercession, of praise, worship, revelation, knowledge or of wisdom etc.

Spiritual rooms contain substance and effectiveness that you bring down onto this earth when you have lingered in them.

Furthermore, there is the courtroom and the throne room of God. There are rooms with endless power and pure energy – and there are *rooms of miracles.*

Personally, I believe that by consciously entering into different rooms of miracles in the spirit, *different types of miracles* will come forth in our lives.

And as we are nearing the end of the end times, it is becoming increasingly essential for us to understand the importance of lingering in as many of these rooms as possible.

It can also be said that once you have tapped into one of these rooms spiritually, having lingered there occasionally already, it becomes much easier to return there frequently, thus bringing down to earth the miracles prepared in this special room.

In other words, miracles which God has begun to release in your life will accompany you the rest of your life and ministry here on earth – without you having to again and again go into a major battle for them. This is under the condition that you simply stay in faith and continue to step out with God. To perform and experience loads of miracles on a consistent basis is thus so much simpler than we often think.

Moses is a very good example of this reality. God had "entrusted" him with certain miracles to fulfill his commission. He then only prompted Moses to *use* all the miracles which He had given into his *"hand"* to lead the Israelites out of Egypt – Exodus 4:21.

You have to reach out for new rooms in resolute faith. However, once you have been to a certain room it becomes much easier to draw on it again.

Then again, you will often need to "press in" and to resolutely "hunger for" to be able to tap into *completely new rooms* of miracles and the supernatural in your life. If you are willing to use this kind of determination, nothing can hinder you from continually opening up new rooms of miracles in your life.

Let's now nail this down to a specific example. Most of the Christian healing ministries move mainly in the room of "functional miracles", as I would like to call it here. This means, for example, that a back is hurting because vertebrae or discs have slipped or because muscles, joints, nerves or tendons are not "working" properly according to God's order of creation for the body. Through the prayer of the person ministering in healing, those vertebrae, discs, nerves etc. come back into alignment and function normally. Pain and limited mobility vanish.

Without a doubt, amazing miracles happen in this room and in many cases people are delivered from terrible agony.

But there is more.

What about nerves that have not only been pinched but have been *completely severed*, e.g. because of an accident? Or bones that are deformed, thus causing problems (e.g. flat feet, knock knees, deformities etc.)? Or bones that are too big, too small, askew or bent? Or discs that have completely *disappeared*, vertebrae which have *dissolved*, muscles or joints that have been *completely torn*?

Welcome to the room of creative bone and skeleton miracles.

I call the spiritual room intended for such types of miracles the "room of *creative* bone and skeleton miracles" because here things have to be reshaped or created anew.

Since 2010 we have entered into this room in our ministry and from 2013 with an even greater fullness. Some of the miracles you have read about earlier come from this room.

Now here you may enjoy a few more that happened more recently.

Creative miracle – leg twisted since childhood straightens

I attended the healing and miracle service last Wednesday. Since childhood my left leg was a bit longer and also twisted. I was in pain whenever I needed to stand for long and could often only stand on one leg, having to bend the other slightly – a bit like a stork.

God has worked a creative miracle in me and completely restored my leg. I can now stand on both legs normally. My knees and hip joints are now also pain free.

Thank you for this miracle.

C.D.

Stiffened ankle loosened and healed from splayfeet

Due to an injury I had over a year ago, my ankle began to stiffen.

During the glory and miracle service on June 22 it suddenly loosened.

In addition, I had twisted feet and had to walk bent outwardly. As this strained my muscles and bones incorrectly, I developed Plantar fasciitis (severe pain in the heel and bottom of the foot). On June 22 my feet also turned into the correct position and I now walk completely different.

The problems with the soles of my feet started going away within a few days after that service.

G.V.

Facial paralysis completely gone

I am a professional physiotherapist and work in a practice.

A patient came to me with facial paralysis. One side of his face had been completely paralyzed from one moment to the next. The cause could not be determined even though he had been examined by diverse specialists.

Unfortunately, physiotherapy also did not improve his condition. God put this man on my heart when I went to the miracle weekend in Stuttgart so I took him with me in the spirit…

On Monday I went back to work in the practice and my boss (an unbeliever) immediately excitedly told me that Mr. X's paralysis had suddenly completely disappeared over the weekend. She could only say, "A miracle has happened".

Thank you, God. I am so thrilled! C.F.

Foot shrinks

Dear Pastor Georg,

On October 2nd 2013 I came to your miracle service.

For years buying shoes always created a major problem for me because my right foot was one size bigger than my left foot.

When I told you about my problem, you put your hand on the bigger foot and it shrank. After a quick check of both feet you put your hand for just a moment on that foot again. The result is both feet are now the same size. Yay! I am so looking forward to buying shoes again.

Severed lumbar vertebrae restored

Dear Pastor Georg,

Please find enclosed the x-ray showing my restored lumbar vertebrae.

On 15 December 2012 I fell with my back against an oak staircase. Through that fall a lumbar vertebra was completely severed. During the following weeks, I was in such terrible agony that I was only able to think straight after having taken a cocktail of painkillers. As I refused to have an operation, the only other option was wearing a so-called three-point corset. This was supposed to encourage a growing back together of the fracture.

In January 2013 I attended your healing service together with my wife Christine. Even though I was sitting in the back row of the fully packed room wearing a jacket over my corset, my condition thus not being visible for anybody, you specifically addressed my problem right at the beginning. You put your hands on me and we prayed to God. I got rid of the corset right there and then and I could move totally pain-free, meaning I was able to bend down and walk. After the laying on of hands, I only sporadically wore the corset and I did not need any more painkillers.

As you can see in the x-rays from March 2013, the fracture is healed. All functionality is completely restored. Praise God!

With kind regards G.Z.

Healed from incontinence plus a creative miracle on both feet

I have experienced two amazing miracles.

I am a PE teacher and since the delivery of my third child I have had incontinence which was often quite bothersome during PE.

When I was at the healing service in Linz, Austria, exactly my problem was called out and I felt immediately that I had been healed. I have since thoroughly tested this miracle – the problems are really gone!

Yes, and two days ago, I was at the pool. As I was just lying there, I looked at my feet and noticed that they somehow looked different. Weird, I thought, all of a sudden I have an arch, I don't understand (I have had flat splayfeet for 30 years).

I then went to the pool and dipped my feet in to make imprints on the floor. It's true – I have completely normal, beautiful imprints. And my middle toe, which was longer than my big toe, was not crooked any more on both sides but completely straight. I then realized that walking also felt completely different, just through having arches! What a surprise!

By chance I met a sister at the pool and immediately told her about this creative miracle and kept on making imprints on the floor. She also saw that my imprints were from perfect feet! E.

HUNGER AND FAITH CAUSE IMMEDIATE RESULTS

There are many more miracle-rooms waiting to be discovered by you and there are only two "ingredients" that the Holy Spirit needs from your innermost being to catapult you into those new rooms – hunger and faith.

God's promise is there. *Blessed are those who hunger and thirst for righteousness, for they will be filled* (Matthew 5:6). And Mark 11:24, *Therefore I tell you, whatever you ask in prayer, believe that you have received it and it will be yours.* Thus, if hunger and faith come together things can progress quickly…

There are rooms with even greater creative miracle power waiting to be discovered by you.

I experienced this when God spoke to me in May 2013, saying that I should stretch out for "greater" creative bone-miracles, like supernatural growth or shrinking, or the creation of something new, etc. In obedience I did so and reached out for that "spiritual room" in faith.

Actually, I never thought that already in my next miracle service two days later, such miracles would begin to happen. Until that time, I still surmised that a certain time of "spiritual pregnancy" was necessary. Far from it. For example, a 13-year-old girl had toes with different lengths, and already wore size 12 at her young age. It really bothered her and she had difficulties finding the right shoes. As the Glory of God was released in the hall, the people around that girl could watch as the overly long toes receded to a normal length and then both feet shrunk within a few seconds. She can now wear size 10 shoes.

In succession we experienced how people of very small stature grew several centimeters and feet of unequal sizes grew to the same length. God supernaturally created new bones in people who were missing several centimeters of bone in their legs due to operations. God straightened crooked fingers and toes (on 7 people in one single service alone). Ganglia disappeared, deformed ribcages and other bones were totally restored, "protruding" bones were brought into alignment and so on…

And the best news in all of this is, according to John 14, that this room of creative miracles is available to *you* as a child of God in the same way as it is to anyone else who believes the words of Jesus and hungers for this reality – God only has favorites!

ADDITIONAL MIRACLE ROOMS

In the fall of 2012 God led us into several new rooms at short intervals. From these a number of particularly spectacular things manifested.

It began in September when the Holy Spirit led me in one of our healing services to pray firstly for all those who had pieces of metal implanted in their bodies for medical reasons and were suffering from the impairments thereof. A woman who had a metal plate fitted into her wrist came forward. It was easily felt and was causing a blockage in her wrist joint so that she was unable to bend her hand.

I put my hand on her and immediately her wrist joint became soft. The metal plate could not be felt anymore and the restrictions in her movements were gone. At that moment, we had stepped into a new spiritual miracle room. I call it the room of "transformational miracles".

The first reaction of those in the hall was unbelief. I had to ask this woman several times to demonstrate her complete healing until everybody realized that a creative "transformational miracle" had just taken place.

We have to, at first "orient" ourselves for a while when in a new spiritual room – meaning that our spiritual senses have to get used to that room.

Indeed, our natural man will tend to react like that when a new spiritual room opens up. Many people in the audience had already experienced spectacular miracles in previous healing services, but not *that kind* of miracle. In other words, *the spiritual room* out of which this type of miracle happens was unknown to most. Thus, it was necessary for the people to "orient" themselves anew in order to become familiar with it.

Metal (Titanium) hip joints turn into
healthy bone material

In 2012 and 2013 both sides of my hips were fitted with titanium replacement joints. After both operations I had many long-term physical

---

193

problems, mainly pain in my back and hip. I was only able to sit and get up at a certain angle, and it was always painful. My mobility was always very restricted. When I had to go through security at the airport, the alarm went off every time because of my metal hip and I had to show my medical pass. Beginning of 2014 Pastor Georg had a word of knowledge in one of the healing services that God wants to dissolve metal. I went forward to be prayed for. After that prayer, I immediately jumped up and had no more pain! Since then I can do all the everyday things I had not been able to do after the operations, like jumping, dancing, running, wearing high heels and standing on my feet all day.

A little while ago, I was on holiday. It was two flights and the security alarm did not even go off once!

At the time, I had told my doctors, "You will fit these metal replacements into my hips and God will transform them into normal and healthy hips". The doctors marveled and said: "I would like to have your kind of faith" – and this is exactly what happened. Hallelujah! P.

SUPERNATURAL WEIGHT LOSS

In October 2012, God opened up a specific room in the house of the Father, where immediate or sudden supernatural weight loss is happening. In this room people often end up having to hold up their trousers, because they would otherwise lose them. After the end of one service, a woman was not able to tighten her belt enough after a supernatural loss of fat as there were no more holes left. The belt just slid down her body.

One young woman still had a flabby abdomen after the delivery of her child, which bothered her a lot. While she was listening to one of my messages on MP3, she unconsciously had her hand on her stomach. All of a sudden she noticed her abdomen was shrinking right under her hand. It is now completely flat and all stretch marks have also disappeared.

Here is another example.

Muscles instead of "spare tires"

On Saturday afternoon before going to the glory and miracle weekend I had the urge to put on a skirt and was wondering which one. A skirt came to mind that I had not worn for a long time because it did not fit any more. I put it on and thought to myself, "This is really tight. Should I really do this or not rather wear some pants." However, something in me convinced me to put it on. In the meantime, I now know why this was so important to God because when Pastor Georg said that we could release supernatural weight loss now and asked who wanted it, I jumped up immediately, indicating that I wanted this. I then saw another woman pulling at her pants, looking very happy. I then put my hands on my waistband as well and I was so surprised because my waistband became looser! I went into the aisle and my belly got even thinner. My "spare tires" disappeared! I now have a real nice waist, so firm! And on the next day I felt muscles around my waist and belly that I did not have before. My belly and waist now look as if I had gone to the gym for months!

When Pastor Georg spoke about supernatural weight loss again in another service, I touched my waistband again because I wanted the last two bumps on my belly to disappear as well. That night I looked at my belly and they had truly gone! My belly looks even better now!

Even my eating habits completely changed. I crave salad and vegetables now. I drink a lot and eat much less! My fear of gaining weight has also gone. Now I see myself as someone who has no weight problem and with healthy eating habits! M.H.

I am convinced that without the manifestation of a measure of glory in a service, miracles like supernatural weight loss or dissolving of metal and most other creative miracles have a hard time happening frequently. Generally, "our faith" or the manifestation of a simple gift of healing or miracles will not suffice in such cases.

However, if the Glory of God manifests we are catapulted into a realm that is way beyond our faith or our anointing in God. The God kind of faith from above manifests giving assistance in the spirit to our limited faith making things become possible that are way beyond our own level of spiritual development.

And so, in this way we just let God do it…

In the Glory, God's faith manifests which goes way beyond our own faith. This is the reason why some types of miracles only happen after the Glory has manifested.

I remember, for example, one service in Austria. After a "round" of healings from pain and mobility restrictions, I asked who needed a creative miracle in their bodies – the dissolving of metal, shrinking, bone miracles etc.?

Several people got up.

In that moment, it felt as if all faith had been pulled out of the room. Everything seemed to tell me, "Now you have gone too far. These things might happen in your services somewhere else but surely not here in Austria." Even my wife looked at me somewhat doubtfully…

But it was already too late. People had got up everywhere in the room and I could not back down. So, in faith, I just released God's creative miracle power in the whole room and at that moment I felt the cloud of glory fill the room! While the atmosphere in the room had been "ice cold" and full of unbelief a second before – now, in the blink of an eye, warm, liquid Glory substance had spread all over. (It is very hard to describe this spiritual experience with human words.) In the moment, I felt this presence I knew that what I had spoken out would really happen. God's faith had come to the aid of our weak faith.

Already one woman shouted: "My shoe grew!" After questioning her for more details, I learned that in fact her foot, which had been clunky due to a chronic disease of many years, had shrunk in the blink of an eye. Before, her shoe had not fit properly. Another person testified that her crooked finger had straightened. In another person, metal had dissolved and a creative miracle on the bones had taken place, etc. At the end someone even lost fat supernaturally.

She had to hold up her pants during worship because they kept on sliding down.

God's Glory is truly the ultimate grace for all our human limitations. When we come to our end and "surrender", God will start in earnest.

In His Glory, God will sovereignly work miracles that will surpass our own imagination and even our own faith. His Glory is therefore the key for the "greater things" that Jesus talks about in John 14:12.

Belonging to this are also all kinds of "dissolution miracles", like the supernatural dissolution of nodes, tumors, ganglions, scars, spots – and even wrinkles. If you are a son of Glory, this room is also wide open for you.

DISSOLUTION MIRACLES

Here some examples:

Supernatural loss of water

For six weeks I had severe oedemata in my legs and water retention in my whole body. Even diuretic pills did not help. On Saturday night I came to the service with swollen legs and on Sunday morning it had all disappeared!

When I stood on the scale I measured a loss of 8 pounds of weight and 7% less water! I feel completely reborn! All other symptoms have gone as well. I have strength, fear is gone. Circulation is great. No more headaches. Thank you from the bottom of my heart! U.K.N.

Large cysts just gone

This morning I went for a check-up to my gynecologist, as in August I had large cysts and strong menstrual bleeding.

After worship, Pastor Georg said that there is a woman who has cysts in her abdomen but when she goes for her next check-up appointment, these cysts

> will have gone. I received that for myself and made an appointment when I was at home again. And today, during the examination, no cyst was to be seen. Everything is fine! Thank God for my healing! R.S.

Another testimony resulting from the "dissolving" Glory of God is the story of a family in which their son was a severe drug addict and was not able to manage his own life at all. Any apprenticeship or further education he started, he would abandon after only a short while.

The father had a surgical scar on his abdomen that was about 2 ½ inches long which completely disappeared in the realm of Glory in one of the miracle services. The drug addicted son who had come along with him saw this and immediately gave his life to Jesus. Since that day, he has totally stopped taking drugs and has, in the meantime, graduated from university with a bachelor degree!

Another important room is the *organ-miracle-room*. From this room healing or the new creation of diseased organs takes place.

God has "spare parts" ready for any part of our bodies in the same way a car manufacturer has spares for its cars.

God is the creator of our bodies and, like Mercedes-Benz, the "creator" of Mercedes cars, has all necessary blueprints and spare parts in stock in the same way God has everything at His disposal that our body might need in case there should ever be something wrong with it. For this reason, I believe that in heaven every organ is available as a "spare" in spiritual form at any time and can thus be brought out of the heavenly realm onto this earth.

The following examples illustrate this.

New Heart

About half a year ago, God gave me a new heart in the service. Before that, I had gone to the doctor who told me that I had the heart of an 80-year-old woman.

Through a word of knowledge in the service, Pastor Georg addressed exactly this condition and then laid his hands on me.

After that I went to the doctor. He was speechless and confirmed that I had the heart of a "young roe".

Kindly, P.

Brought back from death to life

A man had had multiple organ failure. He was on artificial respiration and left to die in the ICU, where I work.

Through prayer, however, his organs started to work again. I laid a healing cloth on him that I had brought from the healing service. He had it with him for 2 to 3 days. On the third day, he was able to sit on a chair and talk to his family. After about 5 to 6 weeks he went back to his regular job – without any impairment. R.G.

Intestinal problems disappear after miracle service

After the last healing service, I was surprised to find that my digestive system had changed completely. Since childhood I used to have diarrhea once or twice daily without any obvious reason … now completely gone!

I do not need a special diet anymore… I.F.

Dying man receives new kidneys!

Dear Pastor Georg,

I have experienced so many miracles through you…

Now, after your wife Irina prayed on the phone for my dying uncle, he received two completely new kidneys from God!

The doctors had said he would die within a few hours as his kidneys were completely destroyed.

When they examined him again the next day, they not only found him perfectly alive but there were also two brand new kidneys in his body! Hallelujah!

I listen to your sermons every day. My heart hungers and thirsts from more of God! E.B.

Boss released from ICU after prayer

For about four weeks my boss was on a long-term dialysis in the ICU. At the miracle service I asked someone from the healing team to pray for him. Since that night his kidneys are working autonomously again, without dialysis. His liver and pancreas have also recovered. A few days later he was able to leave the ICU and within a week he was able to go home. A.S.

Another spiritual room that is very important to me is the room of authority over so-called "incurable" diseases, like cancer, diabetes, Parkinson's etc.

Even though diseases like cancer are spreading like a plague in the western world, we can be absolutely certain that there is no cancer in heaven. It is our commission, being representatives of Christ, to enforce heavenly conditions here on earth –which means, no cancer! In this respect the report of one of our healing team members always impresses me afresh.

Terminal cancer healed

End of 2011 my aunt was diagnosed with terminal stomach cancer. She had lost a lot of weight and metastases had spread all over her body. Together with another member of our healing team I prayed for her and we released complete healing. After that healing service I phoned her several times. But her condition had not changed.

"My Father has conquered cancer!"

She is not a believer and did not want to talk about God. I was very worried about her and researched on the internet about the life expectancy of cancer patients. Unfortunately, the prognoses were very disillusioning. One night I was awakened by a deep and strong voice. That voice said, "My Father has conquered cancer!" A few weeks later I heard that my aunt did not have any more metastases and is now completely healed. Our God is so full of love and grace that He heals people that do not even believe in Him! T.P.

This revelation of God's victory through Jesus over any power of cancer is a very important spiritual dimension for us. When we step into it, then cancer and any other incurable disease must bow before us as we speak in the Name of Jesus. Just be aware of the tremendous authority which Jesus has transferred to you: *I have given you authority to trample on snakes and scorpions and to overcome all the power of the enemy; nothing will harm you* (Luke 10:19).

Many of these so-called "incurable" diseases are rooted in demonic powers. This is especially obvious in cancer as it is the "coming alive" of "malignant" cells. In the same way the Spirit of God is responsible that all the cells we need to live grow and flourish in our bodies, a demonic spirit is usually responsible for the growth and thriving of cells that destroy our lives if we are diagnosed with cancer.

We therefore need to learn to step into the room of authority in Jesus. From there we speak to demonic spirits, incurable diseases and malignant cells and expect without the shadow of a doubt that they leave or, respectively, die.

The following reports illustrate this.

Completely healed from inoperable larynx cancer – neighbor delivered from symptoms of Parkinson's disease

Beginning of March, one of our customers received the diagnosis, "We can alleviate your pain, but cannot heal the larynx cancer – it cannot be removed by operation. You will suffocate!"

In a Sunday morning service, we put a scarf in the basket with healing cloths (*note: this is done in accordance with Acts 19:11-12*) and went to visit the man suffering from cancer that afternoon. We convinced him of the healing power stored in that scarf. He put the scarf around his neck and immediately felt relief. Some days later he reported that he only needed one tablet now. Today he is healed and is enjoying his long-awaited holiday on Tenerife. Within 3 weeks he was allowed to work again – completely recovered!

His neighbor who was suffering from Parkinson's disease saw the healing success. He put that same scarf around his neck for 10 days. The restrictions in his mobility are completely gone. He is healed! R.+B.

A boy healed of leukemia after a dream from one of the healing team members!

I go regularly to a prayer group in the firm I work for. We pray for our workday, for our firm and for the people. A while ago I had a dream of a 6-8 year old boy who screamed in pain. I knew that he had leukemia. In the prayer group, I asked if anyone of my colleagues knew of such a boy with leukemia.

A colleague said that his nephew suffered from leukemia. Together we all prayed for him and released complete healing over him. I went to the prayer group again this week and my colleague told me that his nephew is completely healed! Thank you, Jesus. T. P.

Healed from Diabetes

I have had Type 2 Diabetes for 10 years and could only regulate my blood glucose levels by taking tablets. In the last few months the levels got increasingly bad and I was referred to a specialist. The result was that I had to give myself insulin injections. The prognosis was not good. Shortly after I came to a glory and miracle service and Pastor Georg asked if there was someone present suffering from diabetes. I got up and Pastor Georg commanded the spirit of diabetes to leave. Immediately I felt such an energy flooding my body. After that, my blood glucose levels normalized gradually. Now everything is back to normal! My specialist was totally surprised. Praise be to God! T.P.

Healed from ovarian cancer

I had an aggressive form of ovarian cancer and was to "urgently" receive chemotherapy after my operation. The doctors advised I had a chance to live longer after chemotherapy. However, I refused chemotherapy and asked Pastor Georg to pray for me in the miracle service. The doctors explained to me that I had zero chance for survival without chemotherapy. According to them, I was already on "borrowed time". After three months, I went for my check-up appointment. The doctors told me that the tumor marker was at 36, which is an average level but I wanted to be completely "free from cancer" so I went to the miracle service again to be prayed for. At the next appointment with my doctor, she told me that my tumor marker had gone down from 36 to 7.1. That basically means "free from cancer". According to my doctor this is a miracle without medical explanation! H.K.

At this point let me add that it is never up to us to tell other people if they should or should not have an operation or chemotherapy. That is a decision between them and God. God can heal through doctors and God can heal through miracles.

If a person is certain that God will heal them without medical help, we should not pressure them. Everyone is responsible for their own journey and we should support them on this journey. Philippians 2:13 says that it is God who works in you to will and to act in order to fulfill His good purpose. So, if God really put this on that person's heart to refuse a certain treatment, then He will also bring to pass the necessary healing without that treatment.

It is always the individual decision of each person whether they want to undergo a certain medical treatment or not – and we should not interfere with it.

All that leaders or preachers can do is to encourage people and to teach them to listen and follow God's voice in their hearts. Each person is responsible for their own decisions and for the road they take.

Unless God has spoken clearly and distinctly, it should be far from us to suggest to anyone as to which would be the right direction for them to take with such a difficult decision.

We could carry on with the list of different spiritual "miracle rooms". For example, there is the room of authority over deafness, another one over blindness and eye diseases, or a room for creative tooth miracles. Then there is a room of Glory where simply different creative signs from God "materialize", such as angel feathers, gold dust, supernatural rain or wind, oil which flows from the hands, precious stones that materialize, supernatural fragrances etc. I call this room the "playground of the angels". And here the Holy Spirit helps us to really "be like children".

Enjoy the "Playground of Angels"

Financial miracles are in another room of their own (like the supernatural materialization of money, or unexplainable bank transfers, pay raises, discounts, gifts etc.). There are also special rooms for family and job-related breakthroughs, or for the re-materialization of lost items etc.

This chapter could go on forever, but I would like to finish it with a few choice reports from these and other miracle rooms.[29]

From the room of job and financial miracles:

New Job after miracle service

Dear Mr. Karl and team,

I would like to share with you the miracle, with regard to the acquisition of my new job. Initially, in the natural, my situation did not look good as I had lost my job already at the beginning of 2012. Eventually, I did find a new job in October 2012, after I had sent off about 60 applications, but was made redundant again in February 2013.

As it happened, I was at the healing service on February 6th 2013. Right at the beginning of the meeting you said that I did not have to worry anymore because my miracle was already wrapped, with my name written on it, and that the angels had already taken care of everything. On the next day I was sitting at my computer and felt something in my spirit tell me that I could pick up my miracle now. Right that moment I received an email from an employer where I had applied the day before. Never in my life had I received a reply with invitation to an interview that quickly.

After two interviews with this employer I could start my new job as a project manager already on March 5th 2013.

Sincerely Yours, P.G. (Graduate Engineer)

---

[29]We do not have personal reports for a number of miracles, like glory signs which manifest during services as they often do not just involve single individuals. However, you can find summaries of miracles in our services as well as orally transmitted reports in our online miracle news reports (www.glorylife.de/en/).

Miracle power releases university place

Last Saturday, I was at the miracle service. Since then I was certain that I can count on miracles.

I had applied for several study options. On Monday I checked the status of my application at a university. The results of the registration procedure for business science and law, which I had applied for, were online. These study programs require a "numerus clausus," a certain grade point average to be accepted. I was not admitted. I was number 191 of 234 on the waiting list. On the following day I drew on the miracle power of God concerning a university place. A short while later I checked the university's online registration list again. I had been admitted for both courses! Since then, I am always counting on miracles to accompany me. L.H.

Seed time and harvest

Hi Pastor Georg,

A few days ago I put a certain amount in the offering on grounds of the word that we should sow in faith. I specifically sowed in regard to a pay raise. On the following day I had an interview with my bosses, and they said of their own accord that they wanted us to be taken care of like a family and make sure that I was happy. They gave me another 7% raise for this year and said they would grant me the same amount for the following year. In addition to this, they want to grant me a bonus on certain sales. When I came home after the interview, I found supernatural gold dust on my feet. For me this is a confirmation that we are truly walking on "streets of gold". Investing into the Kingdom of God is definitely 100% worth it! M.I.

Supernatural multiplication of money

I had saved several thousand Euros that I wanted to pay in at the bank. I counted the amount twice and then left to take it to the bank.

At the bank, the cashier put the amount in a banknote counting machine to be counted. The result: 1000€ more!

She counted again: Still 1000€ too much!

So I took the surplus home with me. After I had arrived at home, I counted the rest once again because I thought I had not counted the amount to be transferred correctly. But NO, the opposite – I had yet another 500€.

All in all, my money had increased supernaturally by 1500€.

Thank you, Lord! M.B.

From the room of healing from psychological stress:

Released from the psychiatric ward after more than eight months

A friend of mine had been in the psychiatric wards of several hospitals for more than 8 months with only a few short breaks in between. She experienced her disease as if her head was completely empty but with numerous "spirits" occupying it. She was not able to connect with God or His word anymore. She had severe depression bordering on self-harm, spiraling unstoppably downwards.

On Sunday, April 14th, after consulting her daughter, I put a bag made of cloth with some of her mother's personal items in the prayer basket at church (see Acts 19:11-12). That Sunday, Pastor Georg prayed over everything in the basket, including the bag, that the spirit of depression must go and demons must flee. Afterwards I gave the bag to the woman's daughter and I knew that the patient would touch the items in that bag. About 10 days later I saw my friend in the psychiatric ward. She was sitting on her bed brimming with joy. Lively and with sparkling eyes she told me what had happened. Shortly after (around April 18th) her daughter had brought her (without her knowledge) these personal items which had been blessed, she was sitting in a certain spot at the clinic, full of the usual heavy and gloomy thoughts that were going around in circles in her mind. All of a sudden she felt her head becoming light.

These "spirits" were literally "falling off" of her. The next day she went outside the clinic for the first time and bought herself some new clothes. Since that day she has come alive again, goes shopping regularly by herself, reads the Word of God and is allowed to go back home now. She is completely transformed, totally happy and thankful beyond words! E.A.

From the room of healing of specific diseases:

A new life

In September 2009 I got an inflammation on the sole of my right foot. It steadily grew worse. In addition, my leg swelled up to the knee. The foot and the leg first turned red then purple. I was diagnosed with Sudeck's disease. I was not able to live a normal life any more. Everyday things like shopping or cleaning had become impossible due to the severe pain.

In August of 2010, I met two people from the church who prayed for me. The swelling and the inflammation receded drastically. Shortly after, I went to be prayed for again at the healing service and now I am completely healed! I am so happy and thankful for being healed supernaturally by God. I really enjoy my new life! T.P.

Healed from shingles

Hello my Dears!

Since July 11th 2016 I suffered from shingles accompanied by severe pain!

I also couldn't take the necessary strong medicine because of resulting bad liver values.

During my stay in hospital the doctors took me off all the medication. A blood test showed that I had too many white blood corpuscles.

On Saturday August 20th, I came to your healing rooms.

I lay there and the presence of God was strong. Then Jesus approached me, knelt by me and washed my feet. I could only cry. One of the ladies there prayed. As I got up my back was clear!

On Sunday August 21st there was so much joy in me!

On Monday August 22nd I received a lab result from my doctor showing that my blood count was absolutely okay!!!

Full of joy I can now say "Jesus is my healer and deliverer".

T. S.

Healed from food allergy

A few weeks ago, Wolfgang from the healing team prayed for me after the miracle service. Being allergic to a large number of foods, I had been suffering from food allergy. Generally, if I ate any of the foods in question, the allergies manifested in stomach cramps and diarrhea. I went to the doctor yesterday and he did the allergy test again. There is no more reaction at all! I can now eat again normally. M.I.

After a word of knowledge my sense of smell was restored

I put up my hand in church when Pastor Irina spoke out the word of knowledge that there was someone there who was no longer able to smell being healed because that was exactly my problem. Pastor Irina spoke to the problem in the Name of Jesus.

Since then I don't only smell well but have a very sensitive nose that can smell much better than most people I know!

M.S.

From the room of tooth miracles:

Complete overhaul of teeth

When my dentist did an x-ray, I received a pretty devastating diagnosis. Four of my teeth were full of holes and cracks (from grinding teeth at night) and one had a damaged root. I already received the quote to fix them to take home... In the miracle service, hands were laid on me. Three days later I went to the dentist again for another x-ray. The diagnosis: No holes, no cracks and no damaged root at all! My whole set of teeth is totally fine. God has "overhauled" my teeth! M.S.

Blindness disappears

It was the end of July 2012 when I suddenly felt a burning pain in my right eye. It then went completely blind.

I went to the ophthalmologist who referred me to the hospital in Stuttgart immediately.

After a thorough examination they told me that if it did not get better in the next two weeks they most likely would have to operate on my eye. My husband was quite desperate because he had booked a family holiday to Spain quite a while ago which he had already paid for in full. In my desperation I cried out to God. I then had the impression to phone my friend. She spontaneously invited me to come along to church the following Sunday. So, two days later we went to the healing service and asked Pastor Georg to pray for me. He put his hands on me and commanded the blindness to leave my eye. At first, nothing happened but Pastor Georg encouraged me that even if I could not see yet, it would happen over the next few days. I held on to that in faith and, true enough, my eye started opening more and more. And now I can see clearly again! The operation is not necessary anymore. Thank you Jesus! I would like to encourage everyone to abide by the truth, even if a result is not yet visible. M.S.

After the healing service – eyes, nose and ears – all okay.

For a while we had noticed that our son would always confuse red and green. Even other people had approached us concerning this. A so-called color blindness is incurable. We went to the healing service and afterwards had him examined by the eye doctor. His diagnosis – no more color blindness, everything okay. On top of this, our son had hearing problems and difficulties in breathing (polyps). He had already been operated on because of this and was to be operated on again. We went to the healing service and then had an appointment with the ENT doctor. He examined him thoroughly.

Diagnosis: Normal hearing, swelling of the nose has receded and he is not allergic to pollen and such. Hallelujah! It cannot get better than this. A.F.

From the room of re-materialization of things:

Earrings re-materialize supernaturally

I had taken my jewelry set (ring, necklace and earrings) with me on our summer holiday in a pouch and wore it there. Back at home when I emptied out the pouch my earrings were not there, even though I searched everywhere. I also looked through my entire jewelry box – nothing. Then I spoke out that the earrings would re-materialize again. Nothing happened at first. But about 1 ½ weeks ago, I thought it would be so nice if my earrings would be there again. I had the impulse to check my jewelry box again and the first thing I saw was one of my "lost" earrings. "If one has appeared then the other one must be there as well", I thought. And in the opposite corner was the other earring! My Dad is truly the Best! A.B.

Free from addiction

Addicted to alcohol for 23 years – and now completely free!

In February I mustered all my courage and trust and went to Pastor Georg to be freed from my problem with alcohol, which I have had for over 23 years. This thing starts out as a subtle process and then you need a bottle of wine daily, and even more on weekends – to handle the stress at work, to relax and also because of loneliness. Afterwards you are left with a feeling of condemnation etc...

And now, since the prayer in February, which is now 10 months ago, I have not had any alcohol (in spite of massive challenges, especially at work). I am really FREE! Thank you God!

Even the feeling of loneliness has disappeared. I am doing very well! W.Z.

22

THE GLORY OF GOD AND THE

DIMENSION OF TIME

As mentioned before, signs and wonders happening in the Name of Jesus are an indication that God's Glory is working. You could also say He Himself is actively moving in our midst.

I feel we are experiencing a significant intensification in God's Glory movement. You can see this both in the enormous increase in the number of, as well as in the dimension of, signs and wonders happening. Many churches and ministries around the world are experiencing this in their personal lives and ministries.

We are experiencing an increase of the activity of God's Glory worldwide!

The spiritual "tectonic plates" are shifting globally. God is setting the stage for His last great harvest move, which will bring billions of people into the Kingdom of God.

This harvest, however, is only possible in the supernatural realm, which is the realm of glory where the Holy Spirit is beckoning us.

Therefore, it is necessary that we, as the Body of Jesus Christ, leave our beaten tracks and engage ourselves in the new thing God is doing today. We cannot bring in today's and tomorrow's harvest with yesterday's formulas and spiritual "leftovers".

See, the former things have taken place, and the new things I declare; before they spring into being I announce them to you (Isaiah 42:9).

We cannot bring in today's and tomorrow's harvest with yesterday's formulas and spiritual leftovers.

It is the nature and the task of the Holy Spirit to tell us of *"things yet to come"*, i.e. to allow it to take form in us (John 16:13). For us this means, if you have your ear on the heart-beat of the Holy Spirit, you will never be lagging **behind** but will always be **ahead** of your time. The Holy Spirit's "today" is the worlds "tomorrow". Do you understand what I am saying?

Too many Christians have the vague feeling of being behind their times, or they feel the need to somehow "stop" the changes going on around them. However, the Holy Spirit is not "out-of-date".

Such a "retrogressive" attitude is the direct result of not living in the "now" of God and thus being on the wrong spiritual level. Strictly speaking, we are, in this case, living in the "natural" realm where the Holy Spirit does not even dwell. We perceive things of the world, circumstances, and changes, many of them negative from a Christian point of view. From this natural level, we then try to oppose certain developments – and are frustrated at every turn. We might even finally give up. Why?

Your perception of reality is mainly influenced by the spiritual "level" you are on at that time.

Because with God everything works differently.

True change the way God wants it does not happen on a natural level and, by the way, it also does not happen through prayers prayed from that level.

In the natural we actually try to impact (or should I rather say "impose"?) this "devil-inspired world" with biblical truths and values through human methods. We believe that we can enhance this effort through "prayer", which

214

is actually not really prayer because it is not prayed from the realm of the Spirit. This is how religion works and has no real power and effectiveness.

Religion always operates in the natural realm with the aid of seemingly "spiritual" methods.

Jesus did not come into this world to bring religion so that the people of this world could live more "God pleasing" lives. He came to *establish a completely different kind of life here on earth*, namely, first of all, with His family – that is us, His sons and daughters!

This new kind of life is completely supernatural and those who live in this kind of life are heavenly minded, not earthly minded. They are subsequently full of power, freshness, joy and innovative creativity.

The Greek word for this kind of life is "zoe" in contrast to "psyche" (= soul life) and "bios" (= biological life).

It is a life that draws power from one source only, directly from Heaven, directly from the Glory. Through Christ in you, you have direct access to the fullness of this life.

The God kind of life always operates in the realm of the supernatural, directly from the heavenly level of the Glory of God. It is always accompanied by God's power, freshness and creativity.

As born-again sons and daughters in Christ out of this newly gained habitat, we are called to "make known the manifold wisdom of God" to the (demonic) forces and powers that are keeping this world in bondage (Ephesians 3:10). This means declaring their defeat at the cross and, at the same time, confirming it with the mighty works of the Holy Spirit. *This* will push them off the throne!

This spiritual coup will automatically result in a change of thinking in the people around us. They will receive a new consciousness, open up for the Gospel and, finally, by being born-again will change their behavior. The battle we are in is a spiritual one, not a natural one.

By keeping our eyes on God and His Glory, it will even be "fun" and full of satisfaction to fight a battle we know we will win as we really do not have to keep our focus on the natural world, or possibly even on the demonic forces around us.

The only thing we have to know each day is: What is the Father doing? And not necessarily: What is the devil doing? Or: What is the world doing?

Since our enemy, the devil has been long defeated, we should never give him undue attention or honor and, in effect, power.

Concentrating on circumstances or even the devil would be the greatest gift we could make to our adversary. Refusing to do this makes him powerless!

Don't get me wrong: This does not mean that we are ignorant concerning the world or that we live in a deceptive sense of security. That would be the perfect landing place for a spirit of lukewarmness.

We just have to "know that we know", meaning we have to be fully conscious of who we serve and who lives in us, the Lord of all lords and the King of all kings and that He has already defeated His enemy, the devil (see Hebrews 2:14). Therefore, we should not be overly concerned about what the defeated enemy of our victorious Lord is doing, but rather about what our victorious Lord Himself is doing.

He is doing astonishing things in these days. His Glory is moving like never before in human history and we can be a part of it.

We can be where He is (John 17:24) instead of focusing and worrying about where the devil is.

The following revelation will assist us with it:

Everything the devil is doing since Jesus first appeared on the earth is a mere reaction to what God is doing! It started with Herod trying to kill the newborn Jesus, continued with the Pharisees' opposition against Jesus' ministry, reaching its first climax with His death on the Cross, where, for one moment, the devil thought he had won. When Jesus rose from the dead, the devil had first misgivings that from now on he would only be able to "try and keep up" with God's plan for humanity. His assumption proved true in a terrible way for him when the Holy Spirit was poured out at Pentecost: Now, there was not only one supernatural Son of God here on earth, but thousands – and later even millions!

Consequently, the devil has been busy with only one goal in the last 2000 years, trying to keep the growing army of the sons of God from rising at any cost, from being revealed and effective. Wherever the Gospel is preached in power and the sons of God are rising mightily, the devil consequently reacts. He is not capable of personal initiative or creativity – no, he only copies and re-acts.

The devil is doomed to "try and keep up" with the workings of God. By all his efforts to stop the plan of God, he ultimately only speeds it up – if we don't get distracted.

And, since the day of the Cross, he has ultimately been doomed to actually accelerate God's plan through his reactions. These dynamics will always remain mysterious and incomprehensible to him.

Any apparent defeat of the sons of God will turn into another even greater victory through the eternal resurrection power of Jesus. So why should we be concerned by the wheeling and dealing of an enemy doomed to eternal defeat?

In the last days before Jesus returns, the revelation of God's Glory through His sons and daughters will climax and be completed (Habakkuk 2:14; Haggai 2:9; Acts 3:21; Romans 8:19; Colossians 3:3-4). That is the plan of God, and He is already in the process of executing it. I also think there is a strong possibility that He might be able to complete it in this generation.

The devil feels this and re-acts with things like social disintegration, unimaginable sin, upheavals, unrest, pestilences, natural catastrophes and wars. These are the works of his demonic forces. It is his *reaction* to the plans and workings God is carrying out for mankind.

The Holy Spirit always seems to be ahead of this world-time because He is living beyond it.

But who do we belong to? Remember Jesus Christ is the Lord of all lords and He has already won the battle for us. We are His and our one reason to live on this earth is to observe what the Lord is doing and become part of it. There is no need for us to react to the re-actions of the devil!

There is nothing the devil would like more than to try and distract us from being active at God's level and to bring us down to his level or the level of mere sense knowledge from where we would be completely powerless against him.

At the same time, the devil knows that he has absolutely no power if we won't be distracted by his craftiness, keeping our eyes fastened on God, His Glory and what the Holy Spirit is doing. So, this means that we let ourselves be inspired from the source, which is His Spirit in us, and we act out of its flow.

There is nothing worse for the eternal "loser" than being ignored whilst we do "our thing" with God from the heavenly realms of glory. He knows he has no antidote for it.

From the moment we spend more time listening to what the Holy Spirit has to say and, respectively, from where and in which way the Glory of God is moving, we will suddenly realize that instead of keeping up with "our time" we are *already* actually *ahead.*

The Holy Spirit is creating through us tomorrow's world from out of eternity.

Together with the Holy Spirit operating from out of God's Glory, we are setting the standard for tomorrow's world.

That is the truth and that is our mission!

Your *natural* man cannot grasp this reality of God and what He is doing (1 Corinthians 2:14). That's why we do not need to attempt it on that level. Our renewed, spiritual inner man has received the mind of Christ (1 Corinthians 2:16) and thus has a direct link to the plans and heartbeat of God for these times!

RECOGNIZING THE "NEW"

See, I am doing a new thing! Now it springs up; do you not perceive it?
Isaiah 43:19a

Yes, you recognize God's "new thing" at that moment when you completely focus on God and no longer on the natural realm, or rather the territory that is presently still under the devil's dominion!

And when you discern what God is doing, you step into a completely new spiritual realm, far above earthly dimensions. In effect this means a realm that is above the dimensions of space as well as of time.

In Christ, we are placed above the dimensions of space and time.

In Christ, you have already become part of the new creation which is eternal and exists beyond space and time. So, the moment you really become aware of yourself being a new creation you are stepping into the eternal realm, you can see yourself sitting in heavenly places with Him and you consequently refuse to react to what the devil is doing here on earth.

This is where your personal quantum-leap happens. It will allow you to walk on this earth as someone living in and out of a completely new aeon.

From an earthly perspective it is the future aeon, from God's perspective it is just the world that has always existed, beyond space and time. In Christ, it is the world that you have been transferred into.

Why don't you just consciously breathe in this heavenly air right now....

The "isms" of this world come and go, but our Lord is coming, and we are coming with Him.

The moment you recognize your privileges as a son of God, you become God's channel pulling the future, the new things from the realm of the Spirit into the now of this world, and it thus begins to manifest through you.

The former German Federal President Gustav Heinemann once aptly worded it as follows: *"The lords of the world come and go – but our Lord is coming"* – and hence we are coming with Him (see Colossians 3:4)[30]

This means the future belongs to the One who lives in us and thereby also to us. It does not belong to any of the heroes of some demonic force which the devil likes to send into battle, no matter under which guise that power might hide: commun-ism, national-ism, islam-ism or by whatever name people might call that spirit. All these "isms" have long been defeated in Christ, and the more the sons and daughters of God learn to reign in heavenly places, that defeat will become increasingly evident in this world…

DOMINION AND AUTHORITY OVER TIME

Sons and daughters of God who move in the realm of His Glory automatically have authority over all levels below that. This includes over the level of matter as well as over the level of time. It is a spiritual principle. That what you stand above of, or you could say, whatever you are delivered and free of, and that which cannot "touch" you anymore, those are the areas you have authority over.

In Christ you have been transferred into this realm of complete freedom, because His love has taken away any right for fear (1 John 4:18). Where the Spirit and the Glory of the Lord is, there is freedom (2 Corinthians 3:17).

The practical outcome for your life here on earth means that you have authority over every demon as long as you remain on this higher level of being free from anxiety and fear.

You have authority over that which you are free of.

You have authority over every circumstance when you rise above it in the spirit so that it can't touch you.

---

[30] *When Christ, who is your life, appears, then you also will appear with him in glory.*

You have authority over matter if you do not focus on the natural but live according to the spiritual reality of being in Christ (here lies the key to creative miracles!).

The same applies in regard to your authority over the dimension of time at the moment you let yourself be transferred from the realm of natural creation into the realm of Glory, which is beyond space and time.

Since the beginning of time, "dominion" was and is our calling and purpose (Genesis 1:26-28). Man only really becomes what he should be in the eyes of God once he takes this seriously.

Dominion was and is the eternal purpose of mankind.

What is man that You are mindful of him, And the son of [earthborn] man that You care for him? Yet You have made him a little lower than God, And You have crowned him with glory and honor. You made him to have dominion over the works of Your hands; You have put all things under his feet. (Psalms 8:5-7 Amp.)

What are the works of God's hands? Let's read the creation account. They are all listed here: On the one hand, there is the lifeless material world with all its facets and then there are the countless creatures like fish, birds, terrestrial animals and, finally, man himself.

And then, there is time.

Time? Yes, really! In Genesis 1:14 we read: *And God said, Let there be lights in the vault of the sky to separate the day from the night, and let them serve as signs to mark sacred times, and days and years...*

God only made the dimension of time on the 4th day of creation. Although He Himself has always lived and lives beyond the dimension of time, He deemed it appropriate to not only embed His creation into three dimensions of space but also into the dimension of time.

If God looks at time from His perspective it would be like us looking at a three-dimensional object. We could look at it from all sides and measure it, we could move it from one place to another; by using the right amount of force

221

we could warp, expand, or compress it, or we could also place and move other objects on top of its surface.

God can do exactly the same thing with time. He can look at it from above and "measure" it from beginning to end, He can position Himself on any random point on the timeline, He can expand or compress time, He can completely eliminate time from His creation and He can also move parts of His creation forward or backward on the timeline as He pleases.

> **God's plan for humanity was dominion over everything He created, even time. In the Garden of Eden man lived in dominion, and through Jesus he has been reinstated.**

It is absolutely incredible – as Psalm 8:4-6 says, this is exactly what man was created for before the fall. Created in God's image, he was originally created as an eternal being, living life beyond time.

After the fall, as we have already seen, God had to remove man from the realm of glory. Living eternally under Satan's dominion would have been man's final downfall.

But now we are a new creation in Christ and through this we are partakers of God's nature. This means we are destined to live a new life in and through the dimension of eternal glory and to reign in this "zoe-life" through the One, Jesus Christ (Romans 5:17).

It is not very likely that time will be excluded in this ruling and reigning.

No, I rather believe that we are only beginning to understand what this revelation really means.

A first practical application would be that we realize that the dimension of time in which we live our lives in on this earth has to *serve us* as sons and daughters of God, and not that *we* serve time.

This means that we can take authority daily over the hours of our day and declare: *Thank you Father for these hours you have again given me to live today. I declare that they will fully serve my heavenly purpose here on earth and that I can do and achieve everything within them that needs to be achieved today. I put any spirit of stress and pressure (which is ultimately fear) under my feet and say, "The hours of time that I have today must serve me!"*

Your life measured in time must serve you and your God-given calling.

Whenever necessary I could proclaim the "expansion" of my hours so that I can accomplish so much more in each hour than would be naturally possible. This is execution of authority!

Or we stretch out towards miracles of diffraction of time, where we could, for example, when travelling by car, to be at our destination in much shorter time than would be naturally possible...

"TIME MIRACLES"

A whole new range of possible miracles is opening up!

For example, quite a number of people who come to our services have had experiences of reaching the venue in times that were naturally impossible. One example: A woman wanted to attend a miracle service. She was only able to leave work so late that she had only half an hour left to travel a distance that would have normally, even without heavy traffic, taken her one and a half hours (and the roads were pretty crowded). She was at the point of giving up but something inside her told her to keep on going. When she reached the venue, it had taken her exactly half an hour from the time she left. As she walked in the door, I had just got up to greet the people!

We have heard very similar stories from quite a few people.

The most extreme form of this type of miracle is the immediate transfer from one place to another within one second. I call it "Philip Airlines" according to Acts 8:39-40. Some people around us have already experienced this. Sometimes it also includes being transferred to a place you did not plan yourself on going to. In this case it is most likely that a "glory-component" of a sovereign act of God plays a role in it...

OUR TIME IS NOW

Another implementation, as mentioned before, is realizing that by living on the Glory level we always live in God's "Now". This means we are actually living *in the best time ever* as sons and daughters of God.

This "Now" of God is above the level of earthly time. By living out of the Glory we increasingly cut through earthly time with the heavenly "Now". Thus, earthly time turns more and more into heavenly "time", and is thereby our time as sons and daughters of God.

We have to realize once and for all that the world is spiritually ready for us to be revealed in power and glory – we just have to start living in this consciousness.

If these are really the last days before the return of Jesus Christ, then for us, who are already part of the new creation, this is the best time to be alive ever. The following verse applies to us: *Arise, shine, for your light has come, and the glory of the Lord rises upon you. See, darkness covers the earth and thick darkness is over the peoples, **but the Lord rises upon you and his glory appears over you.*** (Isaiah 60:1-2)

When you are living on the Glory level, you are always living in God's "Now", which is the best time ever imaginable.

However, if we as Christians are still living under a religious spirit, the time we live in will always seem hard, frustrating and depressing because in this case we are still spiritually hanging onto what God did yesterday.[31] The devil however has already reacted to what God did yesterday and positioned his army accordingly, so that power and effectiveness of yesterday's divine movement has already been neutralized. *Full power and effectiveness only lies in the things God is doing from heaven today and now.* In this there is also the *element of surprise* for the devil. Since he has forever only been re-acting, he has never managed to effectively hinder anything God is doing *now*.

---

[31] That is the main characteristic of the religious spirit.

And so, what Paul writes in 2 Corinthians 6:2 is absolutely true: *I tell you, now is the time of God's favor, now is the day of salvation.*

Only when you are under a religious spirit does the time you are living in seem hard and frustrating.

In God's "Now" you will always flourish as a Christian, being full of energy, drive and productivity. By living in "yesterday" frustration, weakness and ineffectiveness will gain ground. God's Glory always lies in the "Now".

Hence the following also applies. Spiritual governmental authority over a region, a country etc. always lies with Christians who are **moving with what God is doing right now**.

Should there be no such Christians (which means the Body of Christ in that region will "lag behind" in the worldwide move of God), the devil will find good opportunities in that country/region.

The devil will always be caught by surprise by what God is doing now, and he has no "antidote" to stop it.

In the moment when Christians get "up-to-date" with the move of God happening *now and today on this planet* the devil is faced with a real problem!

I believe that God is now calling a troop of pioneers worldwide, whose spiritual ear is close to God's heartbeat. They are ready to move with the new thing God is now doing from out of His Glory regardless of personal or soulish sensitivities.

The governmental authority over a region lies with the Christians who are living in what God is doing right now on this planet, i.e. in His Glory!

For them the best time imaginable is *now*. They have realized – I was born for such a time as this and my commission is for today; everything has already been prepared for me by God. All I have to do is walk step by step into my purpose (Ephesians 2:10)[32]

FRESH REVELATION

Another reason that this time is so fulfilling and adventurous for us is that new and fresh revelation is flowing continuously out of God's Glory into the now:

From now on I will tell you of new things, of hidden things unknown to you. They are created now, and not long ago; you have not heard of them before today. So, you cannot say, 'Yes, I knew of them.' You have neither heard nor understood; from of old your ears have not been open. (Isaiah 48:6-8)

The religious spirit draws life from the view, *I have heard this before. I already know this.* At the same time, it rejects what it has not heard yet and does not know yet (because this spirit feels threatened by it).

Paul says: *But knowledge puffs up while love builds up. Those who think they know something do not yet know as they ought to know. But whoever loves God is known by God.* (1 Corinthians 8:1-3).

New revelation from the Glory of God is flowing constantly, helping us to live in "God's Now".

The spirit of a childlike and hungry son of God which is close to the heart of the Father therefore stretches out for the things of God with "unutterable sighs", as deep is calling to deep (Psalms 42:7). A godly spirit does not despise what God did yesterday, but is yearning to live in and through what God is doing today – no cost is too high and no distance too far. He knows, this is my life and everything else is death to me.

At that moment when you enter the spiritual realm of *"God's time"* (i.e. what God *is doing now*), the fullness of God's revelation opens up to you. It is beyond *this* earthly age (1 Corinthians 2:6) and also beyond the spirit of the age, as well as religious spirits. The purpose of this fullness of revelation in

---

[32] *For we are God's handiwork, created in Christ Jesus to do good works, which God prepared in advance for us to do.*

this time is to flow into and permeate this world through you and others in the Body of Christ.

A NEW ERA

In November 2012 when I preached for the first time about the revelation unfolded in this chapter, a remarkable Glory sign occurred during the message. This is the original report which was written directly after that service:

An extraordinary sign occurred on Sunday, November 18th, during the miracle service in Stuttgart: Pastor Georg preached about having authority over time in the dimension of the Spirit, which is the Glory of God. He used some Biblical examples and encouraged the congregation to expect time abbreviation, time acceleration or even time travel miracles as well as physical rejuvenation (Psalm 103:5). Suddenly, and visible for all, the radio-controlled wall clock started "acting up". The clock hands moved round and round, independent from each other, at an incredible speed. The large hand even jumped forward. This went on for about 15 minutes while Pastor Georg had asked people who had been touched by the power of God to come forward. Meanwhile some people filmed the clock phenomenon or just watched it in astonishment. As soon as the last person had been ministered to and taken their seat again, the wall clock stopped at the exact right time. Since then it has always shown the correct time. The Glory of God exploded in the room and many miracles happened. After the service a couple reported that the clock in their kitchen had suddenly jumped forward for no apparent reason before they had left for the service that morning. It had jumped to exactly that time about 3 hours later when the clock in church went out of control! This was another confirmation of God's supernatural move in that service.

About four weeks later, during the Glory and Miracle Weekend, God even topped that:

During the message, the radio-controlled clock in the meeting hall started racing a second time (like at the Miracle Service on November 18th).

After hands had been laid on everyone present the clock stopped again, but this time not at the actual time but four hours ahead. Since that day it goes at the accurate speed but always four hours ahead. This is a permanent miracle because it is a radio-controlled clock regularly receiving the correct time via radio, so it actually cannot be defect. We believe God ultimately wants us to know that He has transferred His children in the Spirit into a completely new era spiritually. It is the era of His manifest and physically visible Glory accompanied with signs and wonders as never before. It is an era of faith and boldness, an era revealing the sons of God in authority and glory, just like Romans 8:19 says.

It is very interesting to realize that according to a Biblical understanding of numbers, four stands for an open portal into heaven, and this is the exact number of hours the clock jumped forward!

As already mentioned in the testimony, I believe that this is, in many respects, a prophetic sign for all of us:

The signs of God always confirm in the visible the revelation which has been "downloaded" for us from out of the Glory.

- A sign that the spirit reigns over matter: What the Spirit told the church manifested on the clock being a physical object.

- A sign that God's Glory is beyond space *and* time. That is why the clock was racing frenziedly for a while, time completely "lost control", or you could say *lost its importance.*

- A sign that the Holy Spirit has opened a new chapter with His church, bringing that which was in the future into the now (John 16:13). That is why the clock finally stayed ahead. When I looked at that clock hours after the "change forward", the Spirit said to me, "This is the correct time!" Yes, because it is God's time!

- That the future things of God can flow and permeate into the now of our time is only possible through an open glory-portal to heaven (that is the reason for the number 4). Through the direct link we have to heaven this is available to us as new creations in Christ and we can take advantage of it.

It might be interesting to observe that following those two impressive signs, for weeks and months after (actually, until today) the same type of miracle has happened time and again to people in our community: On a bedroom alarm clock, on a kitchen wall clock etc. In most cases the clocks jumped four hours ahead and then continued running normally. In many cases the duplication of this miracle happened at more or less the same time as it did in the church.

After all this I think it is safe to say that God really wants to speak to us in regard to the dimension of time!

GOING BACK IN TIME AND SUPERNATURAL REJUVENATION

If the realm of Glory has dominion over time, additional consequences follow. We have experienced, for example, how we can "repossess" time for individuals who have lived through traumatic experiences or physical illnesses.

For example, if an individual has experienced an emotional trauma (like abuse), we can spiritually, in the name of Jesus, take that part of the soul which has stored the trauma back on the timeline of their life to before the occurrence of the abuse. This basically means that the soul then goes back to a state as if the abuse had never happened. In the moment that this becomes reality, a deliverance takes place leaving no trace of the traumatic happening.

After having prayed with dozens of people in this manner we have experienced that it really works.

In the realm of glory it is possible to take individuals back in the realm of time to release healing for their souls or their bodies.

Later, these individuals testify to a lasting sensation of freedom they have never known since their traumatic experience. Some say it is as if a large space in them has become completely free. They still remember having experienced the trauma in their lives, but now it is as if it had happened to another person. This means the emotional memory stored in their soul has been completely erased. Needless to say, those having experienced such an amazing deliverance also take a giant leap forward in their faith and spiritual life...

In the realm of Glory, the same thing applies to physical illnesses. Please understand that we are only at the beginning and still need to attain a lot more experience to understand more accurately the guidance of the Holy Spirit in this matter.

The fact remains that a number of people who had been in an accident many years before and were, as a result, suffering physically, were healed in that moment when we, in the realm of Glory, took their bodies back to the time in their lives before the accident and repossessed it.

This also seems to work with illnesses and infirmities which have not been caused by an accident. Many times in our ministry we have seen e.g. how people were healed from the so-called "carpal tunnel syndrome" after we had taken their wrists back to a point in time before the symptoms first appeared.

Here is another example: One lady had had a viral infection 57 years ago when she was still a child. As a result her cervical spine was bent. In the name of Jesus, I took her cervical spine back 57 years in time in the spirit and a few days later she reported that her cervical spine had completely straightened out. I believe that such miracles will increasingly occur in the future through the sons and daughters of God worldwide.

Let us look at the following scripture in Psalm 103, verses 1 to 5:

*Praise the Lord, my soul; all my inmost being, praise his holy name. Praise the Lord, my soul, and forget not all his benefits – who forgives all your sins and heals all your diseases, who redeems your life from the pit and crowns you with love and compassion, who satisfies your desires with good things so that **your youth is renewed like the eagle's**.*

How many times have we quoted the first four and a half verses of this Psalm, thus emphasizing that God's work of redemption includes firstly forgiveness of sin, secondly healing from sickness, thirdly deliverance from bondage and burdens and, fourthly, prosperity in all aspects of your life, including the material ones.

And this is absolutely correct!

But why have we never taken the second part of verse 5 into this list? *Your youth is renewed like the eagle's.*

Why should it be so absurd that we, being a brand new creation in the spirit should have access in the realm of glory to the sources of supernatural rejuvenation for body and soul? After all, Psalm 103 prophesies our redemption through Jesus!

Psalm 103 prophesies our redemption through Jesus and includes supernatural rejuvenation.

Basically all of the above mentioned testimonies concerning deliverance from emotional or physical traumas of the past are just part of the fulfillment of this prophecy...

And it's also a fact that we have heard testimonies from some people who, after listening to a sermon, discovered that certain wrinkles in their faces that had bothered them had just disappeared.

Others report that their already lost hair grew again, sometimes even stronger and more beautiful than before.

I am not speaking in favor of any worldly obsession with youthfulness but these testimonies are at least signs to point out that we can take Psalm 103:5 quite literally. Through Jesus we have received dominion over time in the realm of Glory and, under the leadership of the Holy Spirit, it may also be applied in this above sense.

I do not believe that the main focus of our ministry should be on the outward rejuvenation of people. Being a new creation, every son and daughter of God has been equipped with an inner beauty which by far outshines any outward blemish (flaw) from a worldly point of view.

But why should we not trust God that He would in His love also endow us with such signs of His favor and make room for Him in this respect?

Likewise, in this context, it is also interesting to see that miracles of weight-loss, which take the same line, and which I also mentioned in an earlier chapter, result in a completely new attitude by the person in regard to their body. Some, for instance, testified that by losing weight supernaturally the fear of becoming too fat disappeared or, alternatively, the experience was accompanied with a new acceptance of their body, even though they were still overweight!

This means that God did not just take a few pounds off these people (mostly women) but planted into their hearts a consciousness of being wonderfully and beautifully made, telling them, "I love you just the way you are, so you can also love yourself!"

God restores the consciousness of your beauty from the inside out.

It truly is a twofold miracle from God if, with "erasing" some visible signs of ageing, a similar thinking of being beautifully made is implanted into us.

One thing I know for certain, we have, at this point of time, only grasped a small part of this revelation of what God has prepared for us in the realm of Glory with regard to dealing with time.

Being pioneers in the spirit, there is much waiting to be discovered for you and me!

PART V

AN ARMY IS RISING

23

THE SPIRIT OF SONSHIP AND

THE ARMY OF THE LORD

About three years ago, I was in the Glory prostrate on the floor in my office having fellowship with God. As I was praising God's greatness and holiness, suddenly a spiritual "film clip" once again played before my eyes. *In the Spirit I saw a large crowd of people rising up all over the world in holiness, clarity and determination for God and His order, for Jesus and His Gospel, completely reshaping human culture afresh. Something entirely new was rising up in the Spirit, and a total change of the current social circumstances towards God's values and standards followed.*

The army of the glorified church is rising in the midst of growing outer darkness.

I believe with all my heart that we are racing in long strides towards the last act of God's redemption plan.

The glorious and increasingly "glorified" church is rising up in the midst of growing outer darkness. It will meet the returning Lord, prepare His coming and finally receive Him when He returns in all His Power and Glory, ending this current world age.

In the center of the great drama which is now beginning to unfold you won't find worldly politicians or global economic players – it will be you and me, the sons and daughters in Christ.

THE SPIRIT OF SONSHIP AND THE ARMY OF THE LORD

The Spirit you received does not make you slaves, so that you live in fear again; rather, the Spirit you received brought about your adoption to sonship. And by him we cry, Abba, Father. (Romans 8:15)

The results of the new creation through the Holy Spirit are the sons and daughters of God – created in the same image and nature as Jesus, the Firstborn Son of God.

For those God foreknew he also predestined to be conformed to the image of his Son, that he might be the firstborn among many brothers and sisters. And those he predestined, he also called; those he called, he also justified; those he justified, he also glorified. (Romans 8:29-30)

What a mind-blowing statement!

In actual fact, in all of God's creation, be it in the seen or the unseen world, there is no higher being, except God, than a son of God. At the moment, the angels still have more power and glory than we do here on earth because they live constantly in God's untainted Glory. At the same time, Paul writes that we, the sons of God, will even judge angels one day (1 Corinthians 6:3)!

There is no higher being in all of creation than a son of God!

From the very beginning mankind was the crown of creation. Created as a spiritual being in the image of God, mankind was destined to live as a son of God *(I said, 'You are "gods"; you are all sons of the Most High.' (*Psalms 82:6))

The work Jesus accomplished in actual fact laid the foundation for us to become real, direct and perfect sons and daughters of God.

"...In this world we are like Jesus." (1 John 4:17)

The prerequisite for this is that a completely new spirit has taken residence in us. Romans 8:15 calls this the *"spirit of sonship"*.

This spirit gives you the liberty to act with forthrightness as a son of God on this earth and to bring down the house of your Father (heaven) into this world and spread it out.

As a son you are the highest dignitary of God here on earth and the Word of God says that creation waits in eager expectation for the children of God (that's you!) to be revealed and become visible on this planet (see Romans 8:19).

This army that is now beginning to rise worldwide is an army of sons.[33]

The spirit of sonship sets you free to be incredibly bold and fearless because you know that the Father loves you unconditionally.

This army is thus a fearless army. There is no fear in the spirit of sonship because sonship means perfect safety in the love of the Father – and perfect love drives out fear (1 John 4:18).

The devil will do anything to intimidate you as you rise as a son of God in Christ. He will try to unsettle you, making you feel "small" and insignificant or try to stop you somehow through any other means. However, you always remain conscious of the fact that you do not have a spirit of slavery but a spirit of sonship living in you and, resting in the assurance of being loved, you cry out, "Abba, Father!"

The spirit of sonship sets you free to be bold and strong. Through this you can step out in faith and determination, knowing that nothing and no one can stop you. If the devil comes at you from one direction, he will flee from you in seven (Deuteronomy 28:7).

No weapon forged against you will prevail, and you will refute every tongue that accuses you (Isaiah 54:17). *Because the one who is in you is greater than the one who is in the world* (1 John 4:4).

---

[33] As already mentioned, the term "sons" includes male as well as female since there is no distinction between the sexes in the spirit.

Joel, chapter 2, read from a perspective of revelation of the New Covenant, gives us a good insight into the army of the sons of God. Worldwide they are on the rise, gathering in centers of God's Glory with the drive of conquering this world in the spirit for the love of the Father.

Blow the trumpet in Zion; sound the alarm on my holy hill (meaning from the position of the Glory of God). *Let all who live in the land tremble, for the day of the Lord is coming. It is close at hand* (when Jesus will manifest in all of His Glory and Power on this earth) – *a day of darkness and gloom, a day of clouds and blackness* (compare Exodus 19:9-16, where the Glory of God is described as a dark and dense cloud).

Like dawn spreading across the mountains a large and mighty army comes (this is the sons of God being revealed), *such as never was in ancient times or ever will be in ages to come. Before them* (the army) *fire devours, behind them a flame blazes. Before them the land is like the garden of Eden, behind them, a desert waste* (in the light of the New Covenant this is talking about the "land" of the devil, not a natural land) – *nothing escapes them* (the army). *They have the appearance of horses; they gallop like cavalry. With a noise like that of chariots they leap over the mountaintops, like a crackling fire consuming stubble, like a mighty army drawn up for battle. At the sight of them, nations are in anguish; every face turns pale. They charge like warriors (German translation: heroes).* **What is a hero?** The answer is, he is someone who puts his life and his own desires on the line to fight for a common cause. In this sense, a warrior is someone who lays down his life because of love –which is God's cause. This then makes him a "hero".

"Heroes" do not hold on to their own lives but lay it all on the line for God's cause, prepared to pay any personal price.

A hero in this sense is someone who is even prepared to do things which might seemingly be to his disadvantage in order to do the will of God and accomplish His goals. The sons of God are willing to do that because they are not afraid any more …*They scale walls like soldiers. They march in line, not swerving from their course* (i.e. they won't be distracted or sidetracked). *They do not jostle each other; each marches straight ahead* (i.e. they are very disciplined, not against each other, not rebellious. No "friendly fire" against their own people. Rather clear focused in thoughts and words). *They plunge through defenses without breaking ranks. They rush upon the city; they run along the wall. They climb into the houses; like thieves they enter through the windows.* Here we see the exact opposite of half-heartedness. A radical determination seeking any opportunity to take the Glory of God into this world – because the time is ripe and hot. A pioneer Christian is not interested in a comfortable, average life!

As a result *the earth shakes before them, the heavens tremble, the sun and moon are darkened, and the stars no longer shine* (a metaphor of the end of this present human-demonic world age under the devil). *The Lord thunders at the head of his army; his forces are beyond number, and mighty is the army that obeys his command.* (Joel 2:1-11)

Can you hear it? The sons and daughters of God are being called now. Will you join the ranks of the army of love and faith, of power and of glory? The bride is rising now, full of joy and with the power of signs and wonders to conquer the earth. She is forming the glorified church and will be meeting her bridegroom, Jesus. Will YOU be there?

Are you prepared to leave the spectator stands, the "sickbay" behind you and make a difference in this world with your life?

Are you prepared to run the marathon, not only a short sprint? Are you prepared to run the race with passion and dedication so you will win the prize (1 Corinthians 9:24)?

You have been qualified through Jesus in you to be one of the sons of the Glory of God who are rising now. You have been enabled. All it takes is your decision!

24

AUTHORITY AND GLORY

A key aspect which helps an army to "operate" in the correct way and gain victory effectively is having a proper understanding of authority.

Since the Body of Christ is a spiritual body, the authority in question is of course spiritual, not natural, human authority.

It is of utmost importance to comprehend the significance of this authority afresh and deeper than ever before ...

I have observed that the Body of Christ in the western world, being influenced by the prevalent spirit of society, has mostly lost the spiritual understanding of authority. Nonetheless, the Kingdom of God is a kingly rule (Greek "basileia") and not a democracy.

The Kingdom of God operates on principles that are in part completely contrary to the principles of this world.

A free, democratic *political* order (at least in the western world) has doubtlessly, from a historical point of view, been the best framework for preaching the Gospel of the Kingdom of God freely. However, since the Kingdom we preach is not of this world (John 18:36) it does not function *in itself* according to worldly principles.

This means to be able to take the place in God's Kingdom that is ideally suited for us and, at the same time be an effective light and salt of the world, all worldly principles and character traits need to vanish out of our spiritual life. With this, we are therefore still able to be active and socially successful members of a democratic society – but we make a clear distinction between our citizenship on earth and the one in heaven.

"Heavenly citizenship" operates under completely different aspects and principles than "earthly citizenship". The more the Body of Jesus Christ fits in with the "spirit of the age", their power as salt and light decreases.

We have to recognize that the Glory of God is the radiance, manifestation and personal presence of a *king* – the absolute and most high *King of kings*.

If we wish to accommodate and carry this Glory in our midst and see its impact in our lives, we need to learn to submit to God and His Kingdom as we would to any king and his kingdom.

A king is an authority figure, not a buddy who might influence us from time to time and we him sometimes.

God is an authority figure – and He is represented by people of authority.

And in the way our King is an authority figure and the greatest and mightiest potentate (of love), His Kingdom operates – in love – according to the principles of authority. Many Christians don't have a problem lifting God high in praise and worship as King. However, as soon as the Kingship of God starts to visibly manifest here on earth, e.g. God manifesting through a person, people have not learned to respect and honor these vessels as part of the spiritual order of authority as the Kingdom of God here on earth.

This is one major reason why many Christians, even though their motives are right, experience so little of the power and Glory of God in their lives. However, it doesn't have to stay that way.

In the First Epistle of John it says (1 John 4:20), *Whoever claims to love God yet hates a brother or sister is a liar. For whoever does not love their brother and sister, whom they have seen, cannot love God, whom they have not seen.*

Here, a basic biblical principle is established: The type of relationship we have with God must always have an effect on our relationships with people in our environment, otherwise our relationship with God is not genuine but a mere religious ritual.

However, this applies to the aspect of love as much as to the aspect of *authority*.

Our genuine relationship with God can always be, to a degree, seen in the relationship we have with authority figures He has appointed for us.

You could also say that when someone says he respects and honors God as Lord of his life but does not do this, in regard to people here on earth that God has spiritually appointed, he is a liar. This might sound very harsh, but in fact this son of God does not live a truly consistent life in the spirit. His earthly life does not match his spiritual life and confession.

I am aware that these statements might cause opposition. But in my experience this topic is too important for our spiritual growth as the Body of Christ to be carelessly put aside.

In this context, it is also important to realize that the spiritual "hierarchy" of the Kingdom of God is not based on human or secular criteria. In other words, just because someone might be appointed for a certain ministry by a group of people on grounds of a degree or according to certain traditional, clerical or even just human criteria, this by no means automatically qualifies this person as a spiritual authority in God's eyes.

How can we recognize someone who has been appointed and confirmed by God Himself as a spiritual authority in the Kingdom of God – and should therefore be respected accordingly?

For this purpose, the Bible supplies the basic criterion of the fruit (Matthew 7:16 onwards). Spiritual authority can be measured by to what extent the *effects* confirm the words a person speaks.

When a son or daughter of God speaks with spiritual authority in the Name of Jesus, this will have genuine and relevant impact on the visible and invisible world.

These effects are produced through the power which accompanies Godly authority. Paul thus says in 1 Corinthians 4:20 that the Kingdom of God is not a matter of talk but of power.

If the effects of the power and Glory of God are continuously visible and perceptible with a son or daughter of God, this person very likely is an "authority figure" in the Kingdom of God, in whatever kind of specific ministry they may operate in.

In addition, the so-called "fruits of the spirit" (Galatians 5:22) are an essential factor for the position a person might have in the Kingdom of God.

Without visible growth of this fruit you will not be able to keep a position of authority in the Kingdom of God, even if the power manifesting through you is on a very high level.

God once spoke to me very clearly and said, "The Body of Christ is my precious bride and I will not just entrust her to anybody!"

For this reason Paul defines for the office of the apostle (which has the widest-ranging authority), *I **persevered** in demonstrating among you the marks of a true apostle, including **signs, wonders** and **miracles*** (2 Corinthians 12:12)

A spiritual authority figure in the era of Glory can be recognized by the confirmation of God's power working in his life as well as by the visible fruits of the Spirit.

In this move of the Glory of God, God will call "carriers of glory" who will be appointed and confirmed in many different ways and different "offices" as direct representatives of the Kingship of God on this earth. They will be "authority figures" because of the accompanying verifiable effects of the power of God as well as of the fruits of the spirit.

God will entrust them with an unprecedented measure of spiritual power and authority, spiritual gifts and manifestations like signs and wonders etc. For the Body of Christ, it will be essential to recognize these carriers of glory and to submit to them as a God-given authority. Of course, God is aware that in this He might confront us with our often contradictory characters, fears and protection measures.

The following simple principle will help you. If I can see (recognize) that another son of God has more of God's power, authority and confirmation in their lives than myself and I have a desire to grow in God, there is no alternative but to honor this person for what he is in Christ. If I want to go deeper, I should "associate with" or "follow" that person spiritually and let him disciple me. This is the only way that God will allow the spiritual substance that He has entrusted to this person to pass on to me permanently.

Incidentally, this does not take away the fact that every son and daughter of God has been equipped with authority and anointing solely through the new birth. This "basic equipment" has, however, great potential for growth.

You might think that God will somehow ensure automatically that the anointing on your life will grow – and that the fruit of the spirit will somehow come forth.

However, if we continually refuse to recognize and acknowledge the people that God has already appointed, i.e. allow them to shape and disciple us, then our faith is wishful thinking. The transmission of authority in the Kingdom of God just does not function with democracy or even socialism (i.e., "we are all the same anyway").

A spiritual channel opens up for the transmission of anointing by honoring and respecting "carriers of anointing".

You will only ever be able to carry as much authority (and "glory" that goes with it) as you have learned to submit to authority in your own life.

Even if I would repeat a thousand times that I have no problem with recognizing the authority of God, I would deceive myself about the true reality in my life if, at the same time, I refuse (consciously or unconsciously) to truly and deeply recognize the authorities He has appointed for me here on earth.

With that said, our differently pre-shaped souls still have to undergo a number of learning processes. However, I believe the Holy Spirit will help us with this!

In this context it is also crucial to understand that this principle is valid independent of the "earthen vessel", which is often implied prematurely.

It says in 2 Corinthians 4:7 that we have this treasure in "earthen vessels" or "jars of clay" – and that is true. There has never been and will never be another authority figure besides Jesus Himself who has been *perfectly* in tune and focused on God in every area of life. This means that if we want to we will always find faults and little carnal weaknesses even in a person who is used by God in the most outstanding way.

This should not and *must not stop us* from unconditionally honoring and respecting this vessel for "its contents" if we really want to see what God, in His mercy, has entrusted this person with taking effect in our lives. Ultimately, it is never about the person who is the vessel but always about God behind it. However, in reality, the vessel is the point of contact!

You trust in God alone and follow Jesus alone and yet this also will have the appropriate effect through spiritual connections to the vessels appointed by Him!

By the way, there are many examples in the Bible where God – in His infinite grace which towers above every human comprehension – has even entrusted people who have many faults with enormous spiritual power, authority and glory. He is not even prepared to withdraw this treasure quickly although the person has already apparently and verifiably deviated from the will of God for their lives.

King Saul might be the most extreme example for this…

And most likely it is no coincidence that David of all people, had to serve and submit to this "bad" King Saul until the very end. This was in preparation by God for the high office David was intended for as the king whose kingdom (in a spiritual sense) was to endure forever according to the will of God. David had to stay under Saul even though his falling away from God already had been visible for quite a while.

Only because of this, David became the "good" king that people remember him as.

Honoring the anointing is essential, regardless of the human vessel carrying it.

God did not allow David to leave Saul prematurely, nor did He allow him to take advantage of his obvious weaknesses to strengthen his own position. God also never allowed him to turn against Saul or to harm him or wish him evil in any way.

Today, so many Christians run from their training because of the smallest problem that might occur, or, if a (real or imagined) weakness or fault shows up, they leave the leadership God has assigned to them.

They claim they have "Jesus in them" like everyone else and that God will continue to "move forward" with them anyway, which basically is the truth. However, by ignoring the fundamental principles of God's Kingdom they hinder themselves in a deep way, and rob themselves of the spiritual fullness and authority which God would love to entrust them with.

HOW DEEP DO YOU WANT TO GO?

In this context it is important to recognize that there are varying "depths" of honoring, submitting, assigning and entrusting. And you are the deciding factor as to how deep you allow yourself to go.

1.) The lowest level of honoring spiritual authority is probably refusing to go "against" them.

This level does not always come naturally, considering that many Christians still believe they can afford to gossip about this or that leader used by God because he might not correspond with their concept. One day a leader might be praised to high heaven and the next day he might be blamed as low as hell, even though the Word of God clearly warns about this: *"Do not touch my anointed ones; do my prophets no harm."* (Psalm 105:15)

If we want to have more of God's Glory in our lives it is vitally important that we stay away from anything that has the "smell" of negative talk (often the result of being hurt) or from gossip and bad-mouthing. We should instead, once and for all, make the decision to never make ourselves an available channel for negative talk about any spiritual leader.

2.) Another level of "honoring" and "respecting" spiritual authority figures simply consists of talking positively about them, recognizing that God uses them, maybe read their books or attend their conferences, or possibly even receive their laying on of hands, and be inspired by their messages, etc.

Here again, we should be prepared to show this level of respect to any authority figure appointed by God. This does not yet have to be in connection with a deep personal association.

> **There are different levels of honoring, commitment and trust that we can enter into with leadership appointed by God. We are the ones deciding how deep we want to go.**

3.) If God allows you to be a *part* of a specific ministry, move, or a specific church, a certain level of "submission" is essential. This means that you then have to acknowledge that certain things in this ministry or church are done in a specific way because someone in authority has decided it (hopefully in accordance with God). If you continually "rebel" against those "rules" (i.e. questioning them again and again) or consciously ignore them, it will definitely keep you from your purpose in God because, in this case, the ministry you have been placed in by God will have no real spiritual benefit for you.

Without this level of "submission" no ministry or church will have lasting spiritual power and impact (see 1 Thessalonians 5:12-13 or Hebrews 13:17).

But there is still much more...

4.)If you really yearn for the permanent and deep Glory of God in your life, more of the spiritual gifts and blessings which you see manifest, for example, in the life of the leader God has appointed for you, you will reach out for a deeper level; I call it the level of wholehearted commitment or "entrusting oneself completely".

Of course, on this level there are also a number of "sub-levels"...

Why, for example, did Elisha receive a double portion of Elijah's anointing? (See 2 Kings 2:9-14.)

Quite simply, because he did not only honor and respect Elijah but he *served* him and *surrendered* his life completely to him.

This means that Elisha completely put his life and his fate into the hands of Elijah. He did this, knowing that he ultimately placed his life in the hands of God. He trusted God 100% by entrusting himself to Elijah 100%.

If you really believe that God is good and that He only has good plans for your life, it won't be difficult for you to believe that these good plans will come to pass in your life. Even, or especially when God is using an "earthen" vessel to form, prepare and empower you, He (whom you cannot see) will put this vessel that you can see right in your path.

God even said to Moses that He had made him "like God" to Pharaoh (Exodus 7:1). This means that God would not speak to Pharaoh or work in his life except through and by Moses.

Are you ready to trust God so deeply, to surrender yourself to Him so completely that He can (possibly just for a limited time) associate you in such a deep way with a spiritual leader appointed and confirmed by Him? Are you ready to let God use the association with this leader or "vessel" in Christ to deeply mold and change you through his ministry, even down to the most hidden parts of your soul?

True spiritual fatherhood gives freedom without grudging or condemning.

Without a doubt, a positive answer to this question can only be given in total freedom and in the Jesus-kind of faith affected by love (Galatians 5:6).

This then, also means that a true spiritual leader, grounded in Christ, will never force you into such a relationship or try to manipulate you into a deeper level of commitment. In fact he will always let you make your own, completely free decision. This type of leader will not be offended if you are not ready (yet) to go to such a level. He will "release you" at any time when you go back a step or when the time of profound "discipleship" might come to an end one day.

This kind of broadmindedness and freedom only comes with a mature spiritual person who is themselves grounded in a relationship of deep trust and love with Jesus. In the end this is the difference between a spiritual "disciplinarian" and a spiritual father (see 1 Corinthians 4:15).

This planet is a planet of "orphans". Unconsciously, the deepest longing of human souls is for true (spiritual) fatherhood – there is nothing we need more.

Once your soul is ready and is given the opportunity to commit and entrust itself to a leader anointed and appointed by God on a really deep level (like Elisha, or the disciples following Jesus, entrusting their whole lives to Him), you have definitely already received a great and important blessing on your way to greater authority and glory in your own life.

> **From God's point of view, spiritual fatherhood is the most perfect and purest form of exercising authority because it combines fearless love with authority.**

It signifies that you are determined and ready to "forfeit your own life" (Greek psyche = soul) for Jesus and His higher goals (see Mark 8:35).

And it lays the foundations for a deep transformation of our souls and our character according to God's image like He has on His heart for our lives, which we ourselves could never have imagined.

You can actually "discipline" your soul in that direction, e.g. by refusing to allow your soul to make excuses by finding faults in the authority figure or giving in to negative "feelings".

On this level of surrender, a truly deep and lasting transfer of more of God's anointing and Glory into and onto our lives can take place.

God has established this "principle of discipleship" in the spirit. For this reason, we will ultimately not find a true leader who is lastingly used by God that has not let himself be discipled for at least a season (even if some have from the start been given a very strong supernatural and direct portion of the anointing sovereignly from God).

You could actually even derive the following principle from the Bible: The more radically you have been made "a disciple", the more lasting, effective and simply "better" your own leadership will be. As already mentioned, just take a look at Elijah and Elisha, Saul and David or Peter and the first disciples.

You can "discipline" your soul to trust and surrender. This in turn qualifies you for true spiritual fatherhood.

From many years of observation and my own (sometimes painful) experience, I can definitely say that many Christians would experience much more authority, anointing and the Glory of God in their lives if they would just lay aside their independence (with the motto, "Only Jesus and I").

Some have emerged strongly while they clearly associated themselves with a "mantle" or ministry. However, as soon as they "prematurely" left the school of God they completely fell back, also as far as their anointing and fruit was concerned.

And yet others, who had already been in a position of leadership, turned from "Davidian" leaders to "Saulian" leaders due to a lack of humility. A new generation of "Davids" may be "trimmed" and transformed by the challenge these "Sauls" pose. In the end this turns out very positive for the new "Davids" but, unfortunately, very negative for all "Sauls".

In this respect, God has taught me some deep lessons and I have been able to make profound experiences with this basic divine principle in my own life and ministry. So what I am writing about I have also lived and suffered through, and, to a certain degree, also overcome and conquered myself. I can definitely confirm to you that it is well worth it.

As long as our mind has not yet been renewed we often think that it would be much easier if God would entrust us with His power and anointing "just like that" ("He must see that I am ready and that I have only the best motives…"). However, God in His wisdom knows that in truth this would not be doing us any good and, in most cases, it would in the end even destroy us.

No one can permanently stand in a strong spiritual power and glory without having developed a clear understanding of spiritual authority, first of all in relation to our own personal lives, and then, of course, also concerning the sons and daughters of God that He entrusts us with.

The development of our spiritual personality as representatives of Jesus Christ here on earth is fundamentally connected to our spiritual understanding of authority. This means our own appropriation, commitment, our entrusting – and therewith finally our love.

As mentioned earlier, you are the one who decides how deep you go, and with that you determine the measure of your own growth as a spiritual personality and authority.

25

A WORD OF WISDOM

I was sitting at the table in some kind of guesthouse. Across from me sat a woman I did not know. She was telling me about her uncle who used to be a spiritual man. He however "fell" and because of that died before his time. Suddenly the woman looked me in the eye, pointed at me and said with a loud voice, "There are three things to do to avoid falling: Humility, faith and living up to the full potential God has for your life!"

I immediately woke up. It was the morning of the Jewish Day of Atonement, Yom Kippur. I was in a hotel room and I knew right away, God had spoken to me.

This dream was absolutely crystal clear and I knew that what had been said in the dream had in no way busied my soul previously. I myself would have never thought about it like this. I had to meditate on what had been said for a while to be able to completely grasp the meaning and have ever since repeatedly delighted in the infinite wisdom of this encouragement.

Meanwhile, I believe that the woman in the dream was the personified Wisdom of God. In Proverbs wisdom is often referred to in the female form as opposed to the woman "Folly" in Proverbs 9:13. This actually makes sense in regard to the content of this dream.

Anyhow, today I am more convinced than ever that the three points the woman in my dream mentioned are three crucial keys (if not THE three crucial keys) for living a permanently victorious and successful life as a spirit-filled Christian. If we just keep in mind to keep these three balanced in our spiritual lives, it is most unlikely that we can take a wrong turn.

Therefore, in conclusion, I would especially like to call these keys to your attention.

Three essential keys for a spiritually balanced life.

1.) HUMILITY

Humility is one of the things mentioned in my dream which is vitally important for staying on track in your spiritual life. I personally believe though, if even one of those three points is "underdeveloped" in the life of a son of God, there is a danger of him sooner or later stumbling – even if the other two things are well developed. Concerning humility, the Bible is very clear and direct, as it says in Proverbs 16:18, *Pride goes before destruction, a haughty spirit before a fall.*

However, first, we have to deal with a common biased prejudice. Biblical humility in the era of the new covenant has nothing in common with a sense or feeling of inferiority. It has nothing to do with "not being worthy" or, what I call a religious "worm-consciousness".

In fact, this kind of consciousness is "not worthy" of a son or daughter of God, being a new creation.

We are representatives in lieu of Christ, a lineage of kings and priests (Revelation 1:6, 5:10).

As we have been able to see in this book, a representative of the new creation knows who he is and at the same time knows and recognizes those alongside of him. This means that he would not wrongly assume being the only one on the whole earth through whom God manifests in power and glory. For this reason, he will also strive to connect with others who are going in the same direction with Christ – to learn from them if they are over him in the Lord, or to share and communicate with them if they are on the same level. Humility implies the willingness to submit to authority, not only committing to God but also to other people which in turn makes you vulnerable.

Humility sees the whole picture of the Body of Christ. It will thus neither let you overestimate nor underestimate your own position in the plan of God.

True humility enables you to lift up others even higher than yourself even if you might think you have no reason for it (Philippians 2:3).

If you are truly humble you do not look out for yourself but for God's things – because you have died with Christ. Thus you do not need others to continually tell or show you how great you are and you still won't lose the awareness that you have been made great through Jesus. You have understood who *God* is and also who *you* are in His plan. This then completely liberates you from craving for people's approval.

True humility recognizes who God is, who we are and who the others are.

As you have probably noticed, I am talking about the ideal spiritual personality, which certainly does not exist in complete perfection (except for Jesus). However, we can continuously draw closer to this ideal even including our outer man.

Jesus is living *in you,* and He is humility personified (Matthew 11:29). This means that in the spirit you already have perfect humility.

What else is humility?

Humility is open for true correction at any time, even if it is painful for the outer man and comes with profound change. Humility is willing to be corrected even if the impulse for it comes from other people (not only "directly" and supernaturally from God).

Humility recognizes that you will still make mistakes in the flesh and that true perfection is only found in Jesus and His Spirit.

True humility is a fruit of freedom from the "spirit of rejection".

Humility refuses to use opportunities for self-promotion because you believe what 1 Peter 5:6 says: *Humble yourselves, therefore, under God's mighty hand, that he may lift you up in due time.*

If you are truly humble, no task is "beneath your dignity", while at the same time you can still delegate if necessary (see Acts 6:1-6).

True humility ultimately is a fruit of freedom from the spirit of rejection. This means that you know you are loved, secure and have "a right-standing" with God even if God, other people or circumstances, might question you in certain areas – rightly or wrongly.

2.) FAITH

Faith means embracing what God is saying in His word.

What He says about *who He is* and what He says about *who we are*.

What He says He *has given us* and what He says He wants to *do through us now*.

Faith boldly takes a hold of the things that God promises us in His word. It keeps us from false humility.

Faith keeps us from false humility that continuously says, "I am not worthy to have this or that". Or, "Others need this blessing more than I do". No, faith boldly and fearlessly takes a hold of the promises of God in His word and embraces them. Faith *takes resolutely* – see Matthew 11:12.

Regardless of what I see, regardless of what I feel, regardless of what I am already experiencing or have experienced tangibly, I choose to believe in my abilities according to the Word of God and not according to my natural abilities.

I am boldly walking out onto the water, trusting as a beloved son of my Father that He will let the water (more precisely, His Word) carry me.

In Hebrews 11:6 it says that without faith it is impossible to please God. Then it carries on saying, *Because anyone who comes to him must believe that he exists and that he rewards those who earnestly seek him.*

This means that true faith recognizes God as who He is, namely a rewarder of those who boldly stand on His promises which are found in His Word, given to us out of love.

In Numbers 14:24 it says about Caleb that he had a "different spirit" than the other spies which Moses had sent into the Promised Land. They all had seen the wonderful things God had prepared for them there, and they all had heard the promise of God many, many times that He would let them conquer this land. However, only Caleb and Joshua *believed* in God's promise, only they were prepared to act on that specific promise – even when they found out that their land was still occupied by enemies which had to be defeated first.

This spirit of faith, which specifically takes a hold of the promises of God, seizing God's opportunities and being prepared to step out even if some risk is involved, separates the called from the chosen. This means that only those who walk in faith will actually see the promises fulfilled (see Hebrews 6:12).[34]

Faith always involves risk. The Holy Spirit is however teaching us to *have pleasure* in taking risks while trusting His Word – and then seeing great victories.

Faith is not a work but a gift of God in Jesus. His Word in us continuously stirs it up and develops it.

Faith is not a works which you can produce yourself. Faith is a gift of God which is deposited in you through Jesus when you accept Him (2 Peter 1:1). At the same time, faith develops in us when we hear and receive God's Word with a pure and childlike heart. *(Consequently, faith comes from hearing the message, and the message is heard through the word of Christ.* Romans 10:17)

That is why Jesus says in Mark 4:24: *Consider carefully **what** you hear.* And in Luke 8:18: *Therefore consider carefully **how** you listen.*

This means that it will help you if you continuously decide to passionately and dedicatedly take in God's faith building Word. Listen to faith-building messages, seek conversations that strengthen your faith and speak words of faith. This means make the right decision about "what" you hear.

Also, intensely meditate on the promises of the Bible. Proclaim them aloud over your life. If you need to, hang them over your bed and make them an

---

[34] *We do not want you to become lazy, but to imitate those who through faith and patience* (= holding on) *inherit what has been promised.*

inherent part of your whole life (*Let the message of Christ dwell among you richly.* Colossians 3:16). These are good steps to make sure about "how" you listen to the Word of God.

"What" and "how" you hear is crucial for your spiritual development.

This way you will increase in the spirit of faith and your spiritual muscles will develop, like they do in the natural if you go to the gym, and you will be able to take increasingly bolder steps with God and win greater victories.

God once spoke very clearly to me, *"Never associate with unbelief."*

This means that you should not allow your thoughts and your heart to be contaminated by the words of people who have a spirit of unbelief in their lives (like the 10 spies). Do not allow your feelings to be influenced by movies and media or even "Christian sermons" that carry a spirit of unbelief.

If a sermon ultimately does not create faith in your heart, than it is not a message in compliance with the Gospel because the gospel clearly declares: *Repent and **believe the good news**.*[35]

Every sermon you hear should leave you strengthened and not weakened in your faith!

Train your spiritual "muscles of faith" and "feed" yourself right.

The spirit of faith will keep you on the track God has for your life. You need to make sure to never lose it.

---

[35] A detailed explanation of the significance and nature of true biblical *repentance/ turning around,* which literally means "a change of heart" would go beyond the scope of this book and will thus have to be addressed in a future one. Suffice to say, as children of the Glory who aim to live in the spirit, we are ultimately constantly "turning around/changing our hearts". We leave behind what Jesus defines as the original sin, which is unbelief (see John 16:9), and turn towards believing the Gospel regarding all aspects of our lives. This also includes our mistakes that we actively make (= "transgressions/sins"): as we confess them, according to 1 John 1:9, which means to openly admit them, we receive forgiveness and cleansing through faith according to the Word of God.

So, do not throw away your confidence (frankness/fearlessness); it will be richly rewarded... But my righteous one will live by faith. And I take no pleasure in the one who shrinks back. But we do not belong to those who shrink back and are destroyed, but to those who have faith and are saved. (Hebrews 10:35,38-39)

Faith is an essential key for reaching your Christian life's destination. Through Jesus it is already in you – just waiting to be developed.

3.) LIVING IN GOD'S FULL POTENTIAL FOR OUR LIVES

This point in particular, would actually never have occurred to me as being one of the main keys to keep us from stumbling in our Christian life. The more I meditated on this after my dream, the more its meaning became clear to me:

The devil moves in dry places.

I once heard a preacher say: "The devil moves in dry places." And over the years of my spiritual walk I have noticed that this is true in my life and in the lives of others. It is no coincidence that Jesus was first tempted in the wilderness.

If we are moving in a (spiritual) realm, where we are full of the Glory of God and moving forward mightily in our heavenly calling using the full measure of our gifts, time and dedication to fulfill our destiny, the devil has a very hard time to get us off track.

In such a realm or place we are not easily "tempted" and we quickly spot the devil's red herrings and put them under our feet.

If, however, we constantly choose to live below our actual potential, unchallenged and having relegated ourselves to the side-lines then the confounder (Greek: *diabolos*) has a comparatively easy time to tell us his lies and, wherever possible, keep us from a healthy spiritual life.

Passiveness and lukewarmness are some of the major enemies of a lasting and healthy spiritual life in the Glory of God. You, however, have not received such a spirit!

It surely is no coincidence that Jesus is portraying a very harsh image of what He will do with those who are lukewarm in Revelation 3:16. He says: *I am about to spit you out of my mouth.*

At the same time, He gives the lukewarm church of Laodicea the greatest promise He has given to any of the seven churches in the book of Revelations, under the condition that they overcome their lukewarmness.

To the one who is victorious, I will give the right to sit with me on my throne, just as I was victorious and sat down with my father on his throne (Revelation 3:21).

God has given our lives a great destiny, He *has called us heavenward in Christ Jesus* (Philippians 3:14). But this destiny will only come to pass when we draw on our full potential in Christ and use all the resources we have been given, like gifts, strength, passion, energy and time.

One of the biggest lies in the western world is that you lead a happier life if you do not "have to" work anymore. There is a constant striving for "rest", "time out", "vacation" etc. in our society. On Monday, you are already longing for Friday, and on Saturday you are already dreading that the weekend might pass too quickly and that it will be Monday all too soon. But we can get out of that rat-race by learning to consciously enjoy each day – work days, holidays, every day.

God is not against vacation. In His Word He specifically says that we should have times of rest and relaxation (Genesis 2:3; Exodus 20:8-11). But if we are constantly chasing the next "time out", we are running after an idol and our lives will be thrown out of whack.

Matthew 6:33 says: *But seek first his kingdom and his righteousness, and all these things will be given to you as well.*

Times of relaxation and rest will come to you from God when you always put Him and His destiny for your life first.

This means that God will give you rest, relaxation, time out and vacation just as you need it. It will even find you – if you put your destiny in Him first.

And this means that you draw on your potential and your time to the fullest (Ephesians 5:16). The key to deep and lasting happiness is found exactly here.

And, maybe even more important, never settle for anything less in your spiritual life than that which you actually know is yours, even if it might seem that it is not available or "coming through yet". With all determination in your spirit you need to resist any blockage and any limitation that will keep you lower than God's actual plan for your life. Do this firmly believing God's promises (see point 2) and develop a permanent inner passion for your high calling in God, God's dream for your life.

You are not destined for mediocracy or average – God says, dream big! You can kindle this passion afresh every morning by "dreaming" together with the Holy Spirit and then again and again keeping these dreams before your eyes. You then specifically ask the Holy Spirit what He would like to do through you on this day and you make a list of the things that you need to do. Living just for the moment is for losers. You however are a winner!

You are not destined for mediocracy or average. God says, "Dream big!"

This divine "urge" to achieve something in life has, in many cases, been "capped" or limited by negative experiences, influences and words spoken by others. However, it is God *who works in you to will and to act* in your heart (Philippians 2:13). He, *in you* is what actually contains the full potential for your life and, because you have made a decision for it, it will unstoppably come forth, starting today.

To bury your talents just because you are afraid of making mistakes is not an option for you any more (read Matthew 25:14-30). Those who truly move forward are bound to make mistakes, but that is not a problem for God. No, He has already made provision for the mistakes you will make on the journey of victory with Him.

Giving into the temptation of letting go of the things God has given you just because you are frustrated due to certain developments or hindrances is a dangerous trap of the devil. Possibly "withdrawing" or "dropping out" will cause you unnecessary pain and needless "rounds in the desert".[36] See also Hebrews 10:39: *But we do not belong to those who shrink back and are destroyed, but to those who have faith and are saved.*

If you passionately move forward you are bound to make mistakes – but God has already made provision for them.

Ultimately, the seemingly "humble" statement, "I am not that ambitious" or even, "Cobbler stick to your trade" is just false (pseudo-) humility which the devil uses to keep you at a low level, way under the potential God has for your life. This makes it easy for him to lure you to dry places where you are an easy target.

True humility is taking hold of the full measure of the calling and destiny God has for our lives as sons and daughters of God. It means constantly and passionately reaching out, and in everything aiming to live to the full potential God has for our lives. There is just so much God has put into each and every one of us!

True humility includes the determination not to live below the potential God has for our lives.

It is definitely your destiny to go beyond what seemingly has been predestined for your life through your upbringing, your family and other human influences. Your parents' ceiling (even that of your spiritual ones!) should be the foundation (ground floor), and not the limit, on top of which you build your house.

Everything you need for this is already inside of you through Christ. So now you just permanently stretch towards living on the highest spiritual level possible.

You constantly strive towards receiving more spiritual gifts (see 1 Corinthians 14:1) and to use them in the most effective way.

---

[36]Of course, I am not talking about a divinely inspired sabbatical, a time when you withdraw to a quiet place, for the purpose of intimate communion with God, putting aside all your usual responsibilities for a certain time.

It was an important day in my life when I realized once and for all that standing still is death in a life with God. There is no alternative but to move forward, to stretch out further into His Glory and to constantly take a hold of new and greater things in God and pull them down to this earth.

I cannot and I do not want to rest in or be satisfied with yesterday's successes. I do not want to "retire" to an average, mediocre life, calling this "being a Christian". No, I agree with Paul and also say: *But one thing I do: Forgetting what is behind and straining toward what is ahead, I press on toward the goal to win the prize for which God has called me heavenward in Christ Jesus. All of us, then, who are mature should take such a view of things* (Philippians 3:13-15).

God is challenging you today to enlarge the place of your tent. You are intended for growth, multiplication and expansion.

God continuously wants to broaden our horizon and expand our vision. He increasingly wants to activate new gifts, talents, visions and dreams in our lives.

His Glory is limitless!

And in the same way our possibilities are without limit – as well as our destiny in Him.

The new creation in Christ is created for growth, fruitfulness, multiplication and expansion – in the same way as the first (natural) creation: *Be fruitful and increase in number, fill the earth...* (Genesis 1:28).

Therefore, God is saying to you personally today: Enlarge the place of your tent, stretch your tent curtains wide, do not hold back: *lengthen your cords, strengthen your stakes. For you will spread out to the right and to the left; your descendants will dispossess nations and settle in their desolate cities* (Isaiah 54:2-3).

Jesus has intended for you to bring supernatural fruit. At the same time, He in you is the assurance and the Source of that fruit. Just simply tap into that Source, then "living according to the full potential of God for our lives" is not a stressful and hectic rush or race. Ultimately it will only be stressful if there is fear or anxiety coming into play. All God wants is that we are continuously experiencing the fullness of His destiny for us – living out the Father's plan for our lives. This way we are always moving forward, redeeming our time, passionately and ceaselessly reaching out for more of Him and His Glory – the result being a completely fulfilled life!

Jesus in you is the source of unlimited fruitfulness. All you need to do is tap into it.

Now is the time to rise as sons and daughters of God, passionate about our destiny, casting off all injuries, limitations and half-heartedness and to resist every spirit of fear, inferiority and lethargy. This means we make a decision to never again settle for anything less in our lives than living in the full potential God has for us.

By the way, your age is not important. No matter whether young or old, the best, strongest and most effective time of your life is still ahead of you, otherwise you would not no longer be on this planet!

The best is yet to come – no matter your age.

Especially when the world puts you in "retirement" then it is actually giving you all the more time, releasing more of your energy which you can invest into the Kingdom of God. There is no passive "retirement" for sons and daughters of God. Instead, there is a race we need to run and a destiny to fulfill. And we refuse to leave the race before God's timing, or make ourselves an easy target for the devil by leaving our potential dormant.

Hindrances and opposition on your walk to fulfill your full potential in Christ will only make you stronger and more determined because you completely rely on the power of the Risen One in you. *The gift of God* – Christ in you – ultimately always – *opens the way for you…* (Proverbs 18:16). And this applies to each and every one of us!

26

IN CONCLUSION

Jesus has given your original habitat back to you which God the Father has intended for you from the beginning of His creation – His Glory. So now you can flourish in this habitat and develop according to the full measure of God's destiny for your life.

Through His Blood He has unlocked the door for you, He has given you His Spirit of sonship and now He is inviting you to go on a discovery journey in this supernatural, new world, which is hidden to the natural man who is without Jesus.

He has given you free entry so you can pull all the things you discover in the infinite realms of His Glory onto the earth and enjoy them. On top, you will give others around you the opportunity to benefit from and react to these gifts.

As a son or daughter of God you are one of the key people needed to bring God's plan for this world to fruition and this era to an end. It is no coincidence that God has put you on this earth at such a crucial time and He has given you all the equipment you need to live your life on this earth in the way He intended – effective, victorious and fruitful.

In this, He has destined you to have an essential part in fulfilling Jesus' prayer: *Father, your kingdom come, your will be done – **on earth as it is in heaven.***

Christ in you – the hope of Glory!

A PRAYER OF PERSONAL DECISION

Are you saying "yes" to God's destiny for your life?

If you have not yet made a decision to accept God's offer to become a son/daughter of God through Jesus, the following prayer may help you. Say it loud and with determination. The Word of God promises you that in that moment something great will happen in you in the Spirit. You will be born again and thus become a new creation in Christ, a son or daughter of God (John 3:7; 2 Corinthians 5:17; John 1:12).

So, speak this out loud: *Dear heavenly Father, thank you for loving me eternally and unconditionally. Thank you for sending your Son Jesus Christ, in order to make me a son/daughter of God as well.*
I completely trust in this Good News.
Lord Jesus Christ, thank you for dying on the cross for my sins and for rising from the dead for my righteousness. I now receive Your new life. Thank you for forgiving me all mistakes of my former life. You are my Savior, my Redeemer and my Lord – I entrust myself and my life to you 100%.
Holy Spirit, from today on I will live in your strength as a son/daughter of God. Through the Blood of Jesus Christ I am redeemed, healed, delivered and have been translated into the realm of God's Glory. Fill me now with your power. Lead me on my way to discipleship and cause me to grasp and experience the reality of my new life in Christ in the Glory of the Father –deeper and deeper each day. Amen.

If you have prayed this prayer, you have thus received the glorious new life in Christ and I would love to hear from you. Please write to me at: georg.karl@glorylife.de or via our website www.glorylife.de.

The Lord will bless you abundantly!

Glory Life Network of Churches and Glory Harvest International are the two ministries directed by Dr. Georg Karl.

If you want to contact us or invite Pastor Georg Karl to speak at your event or Pastor Irina Karl to speak or lead worship, you can use the following e-mail-addresses:

info@glorylife.de

info@gloryharvest-international.org

You can also go to our websites on: http://glorylife.de/ or

http://gloryharvest-international.org and send us a message there.

Or you can call us at +49 711 90770910.

God bless you and we are looking forward to hearing from you!